THE NFL'S
TOP 100

BY JAMES BUCKLEY JR.

Thunder Bay Press
An imprint of the Baker & Taylor Publishing Group
10350 Barnes Canyon Road, San Diego, CA 92121
www.thunderbaybooks.com

All notations of errors or omissions should be addressed to Thunder Bay Press, Editorial Department, at the above address. All other correspondence (author inquiries, permissions) concerning the content of this book should be addressed to becker&mayer! Books, 11120 NE 33rd Place, Suite 101, Bellevue, WA 98119.

The NFL's Top 100 is produced by becker&mayer! LLC, Bellevue, Washington. www.beckermayer.com

Design by Bill Madrid
Editorial by Amy Wideman
Photo Research by Shayna Ian
Production Coordination by Leah Finger
Licensing by Josh Anderson

Library of Congress Cataloging-in-Publication Data

Buckley, James, 1963-
    The NFL's top 100 / James Buckley ; foreword by Boomer Esiason.
        p. cm.
    Summary: "A look at the top 100 NFL players in history as selected by a panel of experts, with brief overviews of each player's career and stats"-- Provided by publisher.
    ISBN-13: 978-1-60710-303-5 (hardback)
    ISBN-10: 1-60710-303-6
    1. Football players--United States--Biography. 2. Football players--Rating of--United States. I. Title.
    GV939.A1B825 2011
    796.3320922--dc22
    [B]
                            2011020002

Printed in China.

1 2 3 4 5 15 14 13 12 11

THE NFL'S TOP 100

COUNTING DOWN THE GREATEST
PLAYERS OF ALL TIME

BY JAMES BUCKLEY JR.

FOREWORD BY BOOMER ESIASON

THUNDER BAY
P · R · E · S · S

San Diego, California

CONTENTS

FOREWORD

BY BOOMER ESIASON

Starting a list like the NFL's top 100 one is easy. There are those special players who jump out at you when you see them either in person or on TV. Guys like Barry Sanders, Jerry Rice, Reggie White, and Anthony Muñoz. "No-brainers," as I like to call them. Watching them play is something special . . . and playing against them as I did, you knew it was going to take all that you had to beat them.

So, *starting* the list? Easy. Getting past those no-brainers is where it gets hard. I probably could come up with an argument for an additional 100 players to be included. In my opinion, there were others who could be—but are not—on the list: James Brooks, Larry Centers, and Jim Sweeney are just a few of my former teammates who had a profound impact on the game in my era and yet for some reason are often overlooked. (Just had to get that off of my chest. As a former quarterback, I recognize how vital team chemistry is to winning and to *team* greatness.)

To actually choose the top 100, you have to start by asking, *What does it take to be one of the chosen?* A good example is Muñoz. I played with Anthony for nine years, and I could see every day when we were together what it took to be great. It took, first, a physical gift, which he certainly had. But that had to be combined with the desire to be great, a desire that Anthony had in abundance. He was easily the greatest player I had the pleasure of playing with.

But you don't have to play alongside greatness to know it when you see it. Watching Joe Montana or Johnny Unitas carve up a defense, you knew they were different. Watching Deion Sanders return a punt or interception for a TD was a feat fans came to see. (If you don't believe me, Deion will tell you that himself!) How about seeing Walter Payton or Earl Campbell run over a defender? What about the ankle-breaking moves Barry Sanders delivered each and every week?

Having played with and against some of the men on this list, I think that what ultimately separates the top 100 from everyone else is that they did it week in and week out, year after year.

From Dan Marino to Jerry Rice, the offense in the top 100 is a collection of the most dynamic group of players the NFL has ever seen. From Rod Woodson to Ray Lewis, the defense is a group of fierce and powerful people.

Either way you look at it—by how the players are ranked or by whether your favorites did or did not get included—the top 100 list is a terrific way to passionately discuss the merits of each player. For instance, there are no blond, left-handed quarterbacks on this list!

In a 14-year NFL career, Pro Bowl quarterback Boomer Esiason played for the Bengals, the Jets, and the Cardinals. He is now a broadcaster with CBS Sports and runs the Boomer Esiason Foundation dedicated to helping people with cystic fibrosis.

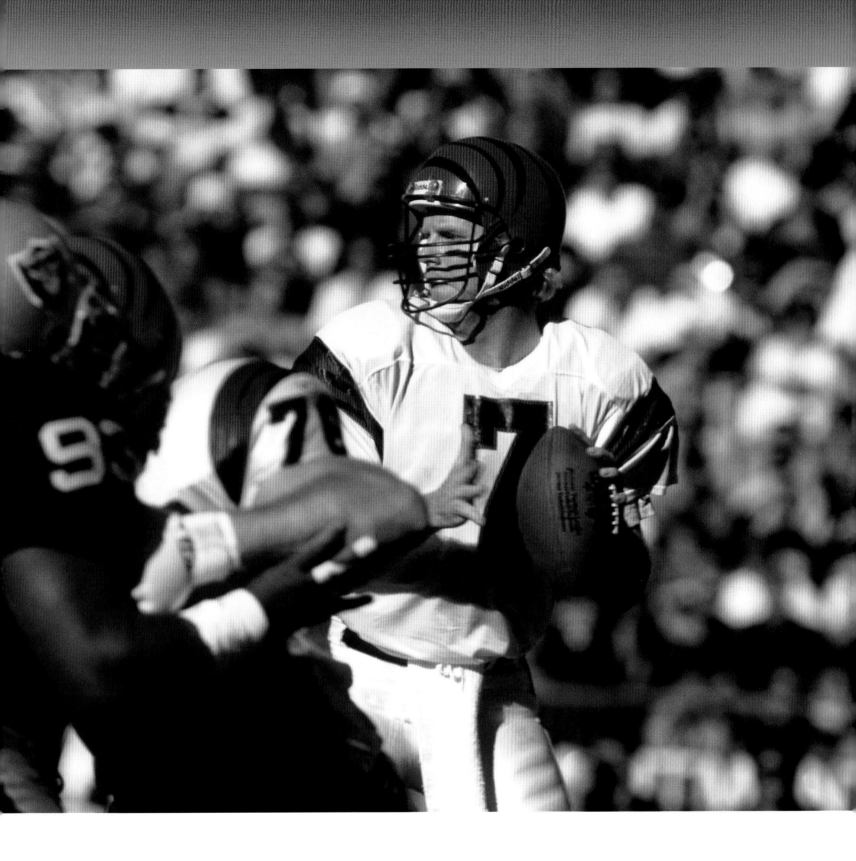

INTRODUCTION

The first games in the National Football League were played, sort of, on October 3, 1920. Surprisingly, no one is quite sure *which* game actually came first, since kickoff times were not well reported in that pre-Twitter era. But we do know that four teams that were part of the American Professional Football Association played on that day. The scores were Rock Island 45, Muncie 0, and Dayton 14, Columbus 0. Two years later, of course, the APFA became the National Football League (hence the "sort of").

Why do we mention this famous football first (or should we say "firsts")? Because out of the couple dozen players who took part in those two games—none appear in this book.

However, in the ensuing 90 years of NFL play, those pioneering packs have been joined by more than an estimated 21,000 athletes. Through Depression, World War, Cold War, and Generations Greatest, Me, X, and Millennial, the men of the NFL have played on, adding each season to a legacy begun by those earliest of teams.

From among those many thousands of players, a relative handful stand out as the best of the best: The NFL's Top 100. We use 100 as the convenient total for the count, but instead of thinking of it as 100, try it as a percentage. How select is the group of players in this book? They represent the merest tiny fraction of all-time NFL players, just about 0.004 percent. Of the thousands of meals you've had in your life, how many

stand out as the top 0.004 percent? We're talking very, very select company here.

The men on this list didn't just rack up gaudy numbers. (Marvin Harrison, No. 2 all-time in receptions: Not on the list.) They didn't just win the most championships. (Charles Haley, most Super Bowl rings: Not on the list.) They didn't play for endless numbers of games. (Jim Marshall, 282 straight: Not on the list.)

To make the NFL's Top 100, you need an alchemic combination of physical skills and mental power. To earn a spot in this august company, you have to stand out not just from the peers around you in your era, but against players from decades before or after you. To make the list, you had to be a winner, even if your team didn't win a lot of games.

In 2010, the NFL Network decided to sift through thousands of players and name those that had such qualities—players whose deeds, skills, and reputations put them head and shoulder pads above the others. The league assembled an all-star roster of football experts from every part of the sport and told them to put their minds and computers to work. After sifting through stats, pondering video, reading clips old and new—and probably having quite a few arguments among themselves—the electors came up with their 100. Fans around the country turned to the NFL Network to revel in the week-by-week release of another

10 in the list, counting down the specials like Dick Clark in a leather helmet to the Top 10.

You'll see the people who made those 10 spots . . . and the remaining 90 . . . but the best part of being an NFL fan is that you get to see some of them again in action on Sundays (and Mondays, of course). Seven of the 100 were still active heading into the 2011 season, and another handful just retired in the previous couple of seasons (Brett Favre and Kurt Warner among them). Watching players like Peyton Manning, Tom Brady, and Tony Gonzalez, you're literally seeing them make history every time they're on the field, adding to legacies that have already secured them this place among the immortals.

And looking around the league, it's a pretty safe bet that there are players who'll have a great shot at squeezing into this esteemed 100 with a few more years of continuing stellar play. (We're talking to you, Drew Brees and Adrian Peterson, and to you, Jeff Saturday and Charles Woodson.)

If you have a longer NFL memory than that Millennial Generation we mentioned earlier, then you'll really dig this list, dude (sorry . . . enjoy this list, sir or madam). Look back with great fondness at the memories of men like Joe Namath, Bart Starr, Raymond Berry, and of course, Jim Brown. And while there are few among our reading public who can say they witnessed Sammy Baugh, Jim Thorpe, or Bronko Nagurski

in their prime, the fact that we're still talking and writing about their talents and exploits decades later just proves how lasting true greatness really is. In 70 years, the Baughs of today will be the Mannings of tomorrow—true greatness that stands the test of time and avoids the diminution of memory.

Is there a player out there who you think deserved one of these coveted spots? We'd be surprised if you said no. The very nature of an election like this spurs debate and controversy. It's all part of the game. If your favorite player isn't on the list, that shouldn't in any way diminish their importance on your own personal list.

With thanks to the electors who gave us this list, and with gratitude to the 21,000 strong NFL brotherhood who has given us so many thrills over the decades, herewith we present the NFL's Top 100. Let the debates begin—and the memories continue.

No. 1 JERRY RICE

SAN FRANCISCO 49ERS
OAKLAND RAIDERS
SEATTLE SEAHAWKS

POSITION: WIDE RECEIVER
YEARS: 1985–2004
HEIGHT: 6-2 **WEIGHT:** 200
SCHOOL: MISSISSIPPI VALLEY STATE
HALL OF FAME: 2010

Even if you never saw Jerry Rice play at the height of his powers, just by looking at the NFL record book, you can't be surprised that he ended up here, at the top of the list. The point of the game, after all, is to score more points—usually touchdowns—than the other guys. Rice scored 208 touchdowns, the most ever. And he's not just a couple scores ahead on that list. Far, far back in second place is Emmitt Smith with 175, 15 percent fewer than Rice. In third place is LaDainian Tomlinson . . . with *23 percent* fewer TDs than Rice. That is what they call, in both stats and football, separation.

Then there are the position-specific numbers. Rice caught more passes for more yards than any other receiver . . . by far (he's a staggering 447 passes, or 28 percent, more than Marvin Harrison). Rice caught more touchdown passes, of course, but he also set a then-single-season record of 22 in 1987 . . . in 12 games! He came through in the clutch, too. His 151 postseason catches are an all-time record, as are his eight Super Bowl TDs (nobody else has more than three). The numbers are simply staggering, a testament to an unmatched combination of skill, training, and the simple will to be the best.

Rice was fanatical about preparation and training, incorporating his famous uphill run into his time away from the practice field. "We'd send guys out to work out with him," said former 49ers assistant coach Jon Gruden. "They'd come back saying, 'That man is crazy.' They couldn't keep up with him."

They weren't alone. In his 20-year career, no one could keep up with Jerry Rice. He could score on long passes or take short passes and lead a merry chase to the end zone. He scored against single-coverage, double-coverage, and zone coverage. He caught passes two-handed . . . and one-handed. He wasn't the biggest receiver or the fastest, but he was the best of both of those things put together. Rice

CAREER STATS				
Yrs.	Rec.	Yds.	Yds./Rec.	Rec.TDs
20	1,549	22,895	14.8	197

didn't just run on the football field, he seemed to glide like mercury through the chaos of the secondary.

He was a record-setting receiver in college, too, but he played for little Mississippi Valley State, far off the radar of most NFL teams. Bill Walsh saw something in Rice, however, and he traded up to snag the young pass-catcher. Teaming him with Joe Montana, Walsh created the linchpin combination of a pair of 49ers Super Bowl titles (XXIII and XXIV). In fact, Rice was the MVP of Super Bowl XXIII. In 1993, when Steve Young took over as the 49ers starter, Rice's numbers, if you can

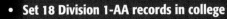

6 POINTS

- Set 18 Division 1-AA records in college
- Led NFL in receiving yards six times
- Named to 13 Pro Bowls
- Had 14 seasons with 1,000 receiving yards
- Had eight seasons with 13 or more receiving TDs
- Named to NFL's 75th Anniversary All-Time Team in 1994

believe it, got even better. In 1995, he set career highs of 122 catches and 1,848 yards (still the single-season record), while catching 15 TD passes. (He also helped Young win his own Super Bowl MVP in XXIX, catching three of Young's six TD passes.) At a point in his career when he was already the all-time record holder in receptions, Rice was so good that he still was setting personal bests. When everyone knows the ball's coming your way . . . and you *still* catch it, that's greatness.

The name of the game is scoring touchdowns. No one did that better than the No. 1 NFL player of all time, Jerry Rice.

No.  2 JIM BROWN
CLEVELAND BROWNS

POSITION: RUNNING BACK
YEARS: 1957–1965
HEIGHT: 6-2 WEIGHT: 232
SCHOOL: SYRACUSE
HALL OF FAME: 1971

CAREER STATS				
Yrs.	Att.	Yds.	Yds./Carry	Rush TDs
9	2,359	12,312	5.2	106

Football is a test of skills, but often it also comes down to a test of wills. In Jim Brown, you had a player who was uniquely qualified to win either sort of battle. Blessed with speed in the body of a linebacker, Brown simply steamrolled his way through one of the most productive careers in NFL history. He played nine seasons, and led the NFL in rushing in eight of them. No other player did that even five times. His career total of 12,312 yards was the all-time best from 1965 to 1984 (when Walter Payton topped it). In the course of nine seasons in Cleveland, Brown started in 118 games—he had 100 or more yards in 58 of them.

Trying to tackle Brown was like trying to slow down a train; in film of him, you can only marvel at both his moves for such a big man and his overwhelming power. His all-around athletic ability was marvelous. Not only was he an All-America running back at Syracuse, he was All-America at lacrosse, too. Some experts call him one of the very finest ever to play that ancient sport at the college level. He also played basketball for the Orangemen.

The Browns made him a first-round draft pick in 1957, and he quickly became a star, winning his first NFL rushing title and being named rookie of the year. Over the course of the next eight years, he forged a record of success and unstoppability that is by now simply a legend. Players from that era tell their grandkids about the day they tried to tackle Jim Brown. He led the Browns to the 1964 NFL championship, and then back to the NFL title game in 1965, where they lost to Green Bay. In the 1966 Pro Bowl after that season, Brown ran for three scores. He was at the top of the game.

And then, rather suddenly, it was all over. Though he was the defending NFL rushing champ and had scored a career-best 21 TDs in 1965, Brown stunned the sports world by announcing his retirement at the age of 29. He had been offered a part in a Hollywood movie,

and he saw another world to conquer. Though his work in movies never equaled his success in football, Brown went at that work—and his community service working with gangs in the Los Angeles area—with the focused intensity that he brought to every carry.

Amazingly, though he had played only nine seasons (leading the NFL in rushing in eight of those), when he retired Brown was the all-time career leader in rushing yards, rushing touchdowns, total touchdowns, attempts, and rushing yardage titles. He also had the single-

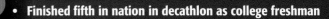

6 POINTS

- Finished fifth in nation in decathlon as college freshman
- Member of Lacrosse Hall of Fame
- Named NFL MVP for 1957, 1958, and 1965
- Led NFL in rushing TDs five times
- All-NFL first team eight times
- Named to NFL's 75th Anniversary All-Time Team in 1994

game marks for yards and attempts. All those have since been topped, but one has not. He averaged 5.22 yards per carry. Among backs with at least 1,000 carries, that's still the all-time best.

For that, for all the bruises he laid out to opposing defenders, for his stunning combination of power, speed, durability, and drive, Jim Brown is the best running back in NFL history.

No. 3

LAWRENCE TAYLOR

(ny) **NEW YORK GIANTS**

POSITION: LINEBACKER
YEARS: 1981–1993
HEIGHT: 6-3 WEIGHT: 237
SCHOOL: NORTH CAROLINA
HALL OF FAME: 1999

CARER STATS			
Yrs.	Sacks	Int.	FR
13	132.5	9	11

The list of things that truly "changed" the NFL is a short one: the forward pass, the NFL/AFL merger that created the Super Bowl, and Lawrence Taylor.

The man they call simply "LT" created such a whirlwind of action from his linebacker spot that defenses and offenses to this day can point to him as the reason they play, plan, and scheme as they do. Some linebackers had blitzed, of course. But none had the combination of speed, power, and drive that LT brought to the field. For anyone who studies NFL defense, there was before LT and after LT. And anybody who had to face him probably wished they had played *before*.

Talk about a hot start: As a rookie in 1981, Taylor—the Giants' first-round draft pick out of North Carolina—led the NFL with 133 tackles, including 9.5 sacks. He made the first of his 10 career Pro Bowls. And he led the Giants to their first playoff berth since 1963! By the end of that season, he had established himself as the premier defensive player in the game.

Over the course of the next decade he would expand that definition to include not just the 1980s, but every decade before and after. Taylor's speed, power, intensity, and technique blasted into the past just about every defensive scheme ever devised. His coaches literally didn't know what to do with him. Bill Parcells told the story of the time that Taylor was twice out of position and in the wrong role . . . but made a sack and then forced a fumble.

Taylor also had a reserve of strength and will almost unmatched on any field. A perfect example came in a 1988 game in which he suffered a torn muscle in his shoulder. Most players would head to the locker room for treatment. Taylor wouldn't even leave the sidelines. He was strapped into a harness and went back into the action. It's

not a surprise by now to learn that he had three sacks and forced two fumbles and bullied the Giants to victory in the game.

Taylor led the way as the Giants won a pair of Super Bowls (XXI and XXV), helped greatly by the powerful defense that he led.

Though he has had some struggles since his career ended, Taylor's work on the field was legendary and groundbreaking. On the NFL's 100, he is the top defensive player of all time.

- Forced 33 career fumbles
- Named NFL Defensive player of the year in 1981, 1982, and 1986
- Named NFL MVP for 1986 (only LB ever to win award)
- Led NFL with 20.5 sacks in 1986
- Career total of 132.5 sacks most ever by a linebacker
- Named to NFL's 75th Anniversary All-Time Team in 1994

"The first question at our team meeting every time we played the Giants was 'How are we going to handle Lawrence?'"

— *Joe Theismann*

No. 4 JOE MONTANA

SAN FRANCISCO 49ERS
KANSAS CITY CHIEFS

POSITION: QUARTERBACK
YEARS: 1979–1994
HEIGHT: 6-2 WEIGHT: 200
SCHOOL: NOTRE DAME
HALL OF FAME: 2000

I n terms of passing stats, Joe Montana is not the all-time leader in any major regular-season category. He played for 15 years, but as good as he was, he only led the league in passer rating twice. In terms of his football-perfect physique, the less said the better. Some veterans once mistook him for the team's new kicker. In terms of fierceness or force of personality or any of the other headline-grabbing attributes you see in superstars, well, he was just a regular Joe. In other words, what the heck is he doing all the way up here at No. 4?

That's easy: He won. Montana took a moribund franchise and turned it into a dynasty. He had help (see No. 1), but without him, the 49ers would never have won four Super Bowls. Without him, his teams wouldn't have rallied from behind in the fourth quarter in 31 games. Though he didn't possess a power arm or a lightning release or speed to burn, Montana was simply one of the best winners in NFL history. Here's a great stat to illustrate that: In four Super Bowls, he threw 122 passes. Total interceptions: 0. That's a pretty good way to become the only player in NFL history with three Super Bowl MVP trophies on your mantel.

Montana started earning his "Montana Magic" label at Notre Dame, capping his career with a comeback win in the Cotton Bowl. The 49ers picked him up in the third round because coach Bill Walsh saw something in the skinny kid from western Pennsylvania (long a cradle of quarterbacks) and thought he'd be the perfect player to run the new "West Coast" offense. Good call, coach. In 1981, Montana's first full year as a starter, he led them to the NFC Championship Game and created the first of his truly miraculous wins. With just seconds remaining and trailing the Cowboys, Montana lofted a pass toward Dwight Clark that Clark's sticky fingers turned into "The Catch" and turned the 49ers into champions. That season ended with the first of Montana's and the Niners' Super Bowl titles.

CAREER STATS				
Yrs.	W-L	Yds.	TD	Rating
15	117-47	40,551	273	92.3

He just kept it rolling after that, not lighting up the stat charts like a Marino or a Young, but just winning over and over again. One point of his play that does stand out is his accuracy. He led the NFL five times in completion percentage and only once in his career had more than 13 interceptions in a season.

After winning four Super Bowls, injuries curtailed his play and he was traded to Kansas City in 1993. Gee . . . surprise. In his first season with them, they were in the AFC Championship Game.

For his innate sense of timing, for his ability to win consistently, and for the leadership he showed time and time again . . . Montana stands on this list as the greatest quarterback in NFL history.

"I would rather have Joe Montana as my quarterback than anyone else who has ever played the game."

— Bill Walsh

WALTER PAYTON

CHICAGO BEARS

POSITION: RUNNING BACK
YEARS: 1975–1987
HEIGHT: 5-10 WEIGHT: 200
SCHOOL: JACKSON STATE
HALL OF FAME: 1993

W hen Walter Payton entered the NFL as a first-round draft pick of the Bears in 1975, few fans knew his name. When he left 13 seasons later as the NFL's all-time leading rusher, *everybody* knew it. And most of them knew his famous nickname, too: Sweetness.

The irony of that name was that on the field, he was anything but. Payton gained most of those incredible 16,726 rushing yards pounding through the middle of the line (though his downfield high-stepping was also a sight to see). Off the field, yes, Payton was sweetness and light and a great smile. On the field, he had an unquenchable will to succeed.

He was a star at Division I-AA Jackson State, and the Bears thought enough of his skill to make that fateful pick. By his second season, he was one of the league's best runners, topping 1,300 yards for the first of what would be nine such seasons. In his third season, he led the league with a career-high 1,852 yards. Against the Vikings that year, he set a new single-game mark with 275 yards (a total since topped). He also captured the NFL MVP award.

Payton became more than just the centerpiece of the Bears' offense . . . he was pretty much all of it. He carried the ball more than 300 times in six of his first seven seasons and 10 out of 13 overall. Payton missed only one game due to injury, and until Emmitt Smith overtook him, his 3,838 attempts were the most ever. Plus, Payton was not just a running star. He caught 492 passes in his career, the most ever by a running back to that point. The threat of his outside speed also gave him an added option: passing. In his career, he threw eight touchdown passes on halfback-option plays.

By the time the Bears put it all together in 1985, surrounding him with a great offensive cast and an even better defense, Payton was an acknowledged NFL superstar. Yet in his zeal for the gold ring, he let his

CAREER STATS

Yrs.	Att.	Yds.	Yds./Carry	Rush TDs
13	3,838	16,726	4.4	110

louder teammates soak up most of the attention during their Super Bowl–winning 1985 season. Payton just calmly racked up the yards (1,551 and nine TDs during the regular season) and watched with good humor as the Fridge took a couple of turns jamming the ball into the end zone. For the Bears, it was a year of domination. For Payton, it was a season of culmination, the near-end of one of the great careers of all time.

Payton showed his true sweet side during the last tragic years of his life, which ended in 1999 due to liver disease. As he faced death with the same combination of drive and heart that he faced opposing defenses, he gave us all another reason to cheer.

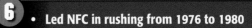

6 POINTS

- Led NFC in rushing from 1976 to 1980
- Led NFL in attempts four consecutive times
- Named to nine Pro Bowls
- Had nine seasons with 1,300-plus yards
- NFL Man of the Year Award renamed for him in 1999
- Named to NFL's 75th Anniversary All-Time Team in 1994

No. **6**

JOHNNY UNITAS

BALTIMORE COLTS
SAN DIEGO CHARGERS

POSITION: QUARTERBACK
YEARS: 1956–1973
HEIGHT: 6-1 WEIGHT: 195
SCHOOL: LOUISVILLE
HALL OF FAME: 1979

How fitting that the man who led his team to victory in the "Greatest Game Ever Played" is also called by some experts the greatest player ever at his position (of course, the guy a page or two back might have something to say about that).

Johnny Unitas (who was always "John" to his teammates, actually) was never anyone you'd look at and say "football player." His shoulders were a bit droopy compared to the Adonis-like breadth of the typical player. He was not exactly fleet of foot. And the black high-top shoes that he wore gave him support, but also gave him an air of, well . . . clunkiness that added to his unusual mystique.

But as any parent will tell their kid, it's not how you look but how you act that counts. And Unitas could throw a football like Mozart could play or Baryshnikov could dance. He was an artist in the guise of a lunchpail guy.

That he came from a humble path to NFL greatness adds yet another layer to his legend. His has been called one of the most amazing Cinderella stories in sports. After his time at the University of Louisville ended, he was in camp briefly with the Pittsburgh Steelers, who let him go in 1955—to their everlasting chagrin. Unitas was playing semipro football (for the otherwise unheard of Bloomfield Rams) when he got a call from Weeb Ewbank of the Colts requesting his services as a back-up QB. That's right: One of the top players in NFL history was there for the taking: the cost of a long-distance phone call. A few games into the 1956 season, Unitas took over as the starter and finally commenced one of the greatest careers in NFL history. Eighteen seasons later, he retired as the NFL's all-time leader in just about every passing category. That his marks have all been topped since takes nothing away from his success.

His greatest years were in the late 1950s and early 1960s. Blessed with offensive weapons that included Raymond Berry and

CAREER STATS

Yrs.	W-L	Yds.	TD	Rating
18	118-64-4	40,239	290	78.2

Lenny Moore (who join him here in the NFL 100), Unitas led the Colts to victory and an NFL title in that famous 1958 game. They repeated the feat in 1959. They lost playoff games in 1964 and 1965 and then won the NFL title in 1968. That was the year of Super Bowl III. Unitas missed most of that game due to injury, but came on late to throw a TD pass in the Colts' 16–7 loss. He led them back to win Super Bowl V two years later, a nice bookend to his early-career triumphs.

Unitas's greatest strengths were amazing accuracy, innovative play calling (no helmet radios for Johnny U.), and a toughness that earned him respect from the fiercest opponents. He practically invented the

two-minute drill that is now a vital part of every QB's arsenal. Among his many records is one that is perhaps unbreakable: From 1956–60, he threw at least one TD pass in 47 straight games.

Unitas played one final season in San Diego before his high-top cleats made their way to Canton. Lots of flashy passers have come along since Unitas last lofted a pass, and only a handful could even challenge his status among the best ever.

6 POINTS

- Named to 10 Pro Bowls
- Led NFL in passing yards four times
- Led NFL in TD passes four times (career high 32 in 1959)
- Named NFL MVP for 1964 and 1967
- Named NFL Man of the Year for 1970
- Named to NFL's 75th Anniversary All-Time Team in 1994

No. 7 REGGIE WHITE

PHILADELPHIA EAGLES
GREEN BAY PACKERS
CAROLINA PANTHERS

POSITION: DEFENSIVE TACKLE
YEARS: 1985–1998, 2000
HEIGHT: 6-5 WEIGHT: 291
SCHOOL: TENNESSEE
HALL OF FAME: 2006

Reggie White was a man who chose his own paths through life. Off the field, he chose to follow God as an ordained Baptist minister, and to speak the truth as he saw it. Blessed as much with a gift for oratory as with a gift for creating football mayhem, he had a personality as large as his quarterback-attacking skills.

On the field, he chose a destructive path over, through, and around the offensive linemen who tried with little success to stop him from reaching the quarterback. When he finally retired in 2000, White was the NFL's all-time leader with 198 career sacks (a mark later topped by Bruce White). Just watching him manhandle a string of Patriots linemen in Super Bowl XXXI is to watch a master class in pass-rushing.

White also blazed a trail in NFL business. In 1993, he was the first major free agent to sign a large contract with a new team. In making the defensive standout the centerpiece of what would become a Super Bowl–champion team, the Packers and White would forever alter the way that NFL teams are built.

White started down these paths in his native Tennessee, where he chose the home-state Volunteers when he headed off to college. He was simply dominant there, setting school sacks records while winning SEC player of the year honors as well as being named All-America. While there, he started his preaching career as well, which helped him earn his famous nickname: The Minister of Defense. After his senior year, however, instead of going to the NFL, he once again decided to take his own path. He stayed close to home signing with the Memphis Showboats of the United States Football League, which would be a short-lived NFL rival. After nearly two seasons with them, he did move to the NFL, chosen by the Eagles in a special supplemental draft.

Over the next eight years, he was phenomenal: In 121 games with Philadelphia, he had 124 sacks. He led the NFL twice in that category, including racking up a career-high 21 in the 12 games of the strike-shortened 1987 season. He had at least 11 sacks every year he was with the Eagles.

After his contract was up, he became a free agent and his four-year, $17-million deal with Green Bay in 1993 filled headlines and lit up the NFL airwaves. Trust us: At the time, that was a whole lot

CAREER STATS

Yrs.	Sacks	Int.	FR
15	198.0	3	20

"Reggie, this is God.
I want you to play
in Green Bay."

— Mike Holmgren

of money, especially for a defensive player. The Packers said he was worth every penny, however, as he combined his fiery leadership with still-outstanding skills to lead the Pack back to the promised land of the Super Bowl. In fact, he set a Super Bowl record with three sacks in Green Bay's Super Bowl XXXI win over New England.

White retired in 1998 but came back for a final season with the Panthers. An easy pick for the Hall of Fame in 2006, he had died tragically in 2004 at the age of 43 of a respiratory disease, with so many paths yet traveled.

No. 8 PEYTON MANNING

INDIANAPOLIS COLTS

POSITION: QUARTERBACK
YEARS: 1998—
HEIGHT: 6-5 WEIGHT: 230
SCHOOL: TENNESSEE

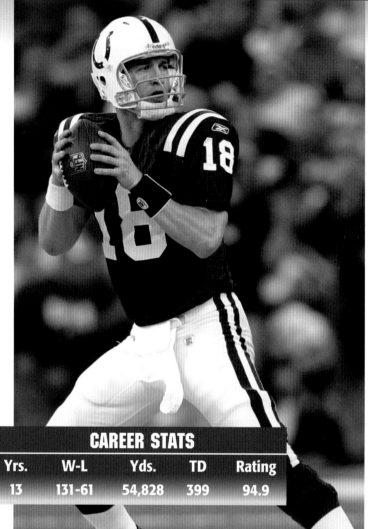

E xpectations can be a funny thing. So much hype and hope can go into a young player that expectations become an anchor that weighs him down. The NFL landscape is littered with players of whom great things were expected, but who could never possibly live up to the dream.

Peyton Manning is the exception.

The son of Archie Manning, a longtime NFL passer, Peyton was almost bred to be a quarterback. At Tennessee, he set all sorts of school records, carried the Volunteers to the top rank of college teams, and just missed winning the Heisman Trophy. As the number-one overall pick of the 1998 Draft, Manning was handed to the Colts and basically told, "Save our team. Make us into a winner."

No pressure, kid.

But Manning had physical skills that let him do just that. And he had mental powers that are pretty much unmatched in NFL history. Manning is a great athlete, no doubt about that, a pure pocket passer with amazing accuracy. The last time he completed less than 62 percent of his passes was his rookie year. He set a since-broken NFL record with 49 TD passes in 2004. He has put together 11 seasons with 4,000 or more passing yards.

But it's his mental command of the game that really sets him apart. His now-famous gestures while awaiting the snap, his ability to change a play on the fly and make it work, his intense study not only of teammates' abilities but defenses' weaknesses . . . all those combine with his passing skills to form one of the greatest players ever at what some call the hardest position to play in sports. He is the only player in NFL history to win four league Most Valuable Player awards.

As for turning the Colts into winners, consider that job well done, too. Manning led the Colts to at least 10 wins 11 times through 2010. After going 3-13 in his first season, they leaped to 13-3 in 1999 and

CAREER STATS

Yrs.	W-L	Yds.	TD	Rating
13	131-61	54,828	399	94.9

earned the first of 11 playoff appearances in his first 13 seasons. And oh, yes, they also won seven AFC South titles.

Indy had trouble fighting through the playoffs until 2006, however. That year, Manning and the Colts were firing on all cylinders. They beat their archrival, the New England Patriots, in the AFC title game and then knocked off the Bears in Super Bowl XLI. Along with the Super Bowl MVP award he received, Manning finally had a ring to add to his many other accomplishments.

And a dozen years after he started in the NFL, Manning is still firing: In 2009, Manning and the Colts won another AFC title, though they lost to the Saints in the Super Bowl. And in 2010, his 450 completions set an all-time NFL single-season record. His 679 attempts were the second-most ever for a single season.

Expectations more than met . . . expectations exceeded.

No. 9 DON HUTSON

GREEN BAY PACKERS

POSITION: SPLIT END/DEFENSIVE BACK
YEARS: 1935–1945
HEIGHT: 6-1 **WEIGHT:** 183
SCHOOL: ALABAMA
HALL OF FAME: 1963

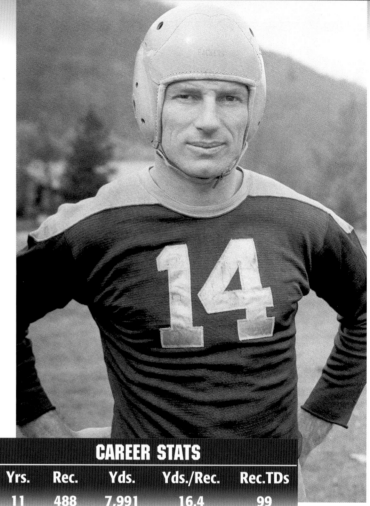

CAREER STATS				
Yrs.	Rec.	Yds.	Yds./Rec.	Rec.TDs
11	488	7,991	16.4	99

Before Randy Moss, Terrell Owens, and Larry Fitzgerald . . . before Jerry Rice, Cris Carter, and Steve Largent . . . before Lance Alworth, Elroy Hirsch, and Raymond Berry . . . there was just one: Don Hutson. Few fans today really understand what an influential talent Hutson was. It's almost like he was the turning point in football. B.H.: Before Hutson, the game was played on the ground, a rumbling cloud of dust. A.H.: After Hutson, the game was played as much or more so in the air, a long-distance ballet of speed and style. (The turning-point metaphor has a nice double-meaning: One of Hutson's favorite moves to get away from a defender was to grab the goalpost, then located in the end zone just beyond the goal line, and spin around to emerge on the other side to meet the pass.) Hutson's accomplishments are so huge that the stats are almost unbelievable.

–9 seasons leading the NFL in TD catches
–8 seasons leading the NFL in receptions
–7 seasons leading the NFL in receiving yards

He was so far ahead of his contemporaries that in 1942, when he caught a career-high 74 passes, the player in second place had 27. That's as if Fitzgerald had 100 catches in 2010 and no one else in the NFL had 37. Impossible. That same year, Hutson had 17 TD catches; second-place Ray McLean had eight.

Hutson's path to his place in NFL history started with his All-America years at Alabama, where he helped the Crimson Tide to an undefeated record and a Rose Bowl win as a senior. In those days before the NFL draft (which didn't start until 1936), Hutson took bids for his services. He took calls from the Green Bay Packers and Brooklyn Dodgers that raised his salary—$5 at a time—to a then-unheard-of $175 per game. In fact, he signed contracts to that effect with both teams due to some communications issues in those pre-email days. The league

office decided that he would go to Green Bay because the Packers' contract was postmarked 17 minutes earlier than Brooklyn's contract.

With his place of employment settled, Hutson got off to a hot start. He turned the first pass thrown his way in an NFL game into an 83-yard touchdown. By the end of the season, his place on the Packers and in the NFL was assured. That year, Hutson's rookie season, one-third of his catches went for touchdowns.

The game was afoot. Thanks to his repertoire of groundbreaking (to say nothing of ankle-breaking) moves and his 9.7 speed (the world record in the 100 at the time was 9.4), Hutson was all by himself creating the position of receiver in football. Over the next decade, he established record after record, leading the league in just about every receiving category possible.

He was also contributing on defense, first as an undersized defensive end and then as a safety good enough to make 30 career

"I think Don Hutson is the most dominant single player at his position of any in NFL history."

— Peter King

interceptions. Hutson's athleticism helped him also be one of the team's top kickers. How's this for versatility? In one game in 1945, he scored four touchdowns and kicked five extra points. Oh, yes, and did we mention he did that all in one quarter? In 1942, he became the first player to top 100 points, with a receiving-kicking total of 138 points.

Hutson won a pair of NFL MVP awards and helped the Packers win three NFL championships in his 10 years with the team. Like the pathfinder that he was, he went out on his own terms after once again leading the league in receptions in 1945. He had other plans for his life after football, and he chose to go out uninjured and on top. For some of his records, on top is where he stayed for decades. His career total of 99 touchdown catches was not topped for 44 years!

DICK BUTKUS

CHICAGO BEARS

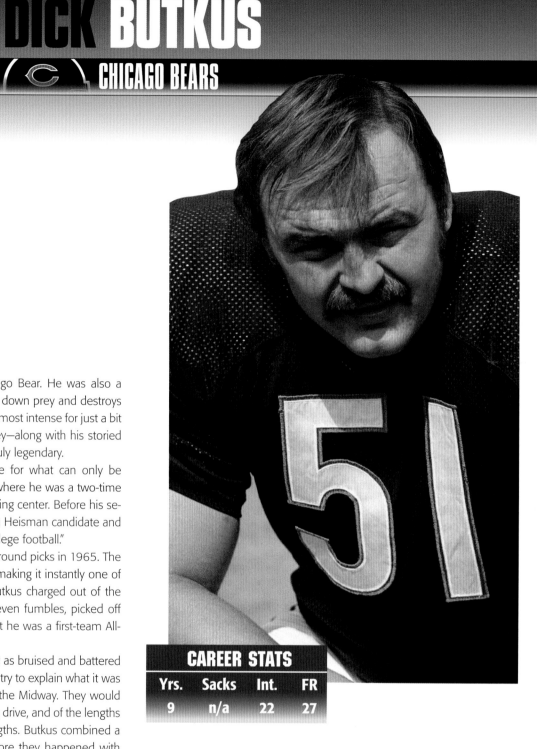

POSITION: LINEBACKER
YEARS: 1965–1973
HEIGHT: 6-3 **WEIGHT:** 245
SCHOOL: ILLINOIS
HALL OF FAME: 1979

Dick Butkus was a Bear, a Chicago Bear. He was also a bear, as in the kind who chases down prey and destroys it if necessary. Butkus was at his most intense for just a bit more than five seasons, but they—along with his storied college career—have become truly legendary.

He first got national notice for what can only be called his Butkus-like style of play at Illinois, where he was a two-time All-America middle linebacker, while also playing center. Before his senior season, *Sports Illustrated* touted him as a Heisman candidate and called him "the most destructive player in college football."

Chicago made him one of their two first-round picks in 1965. The other pick? Kid by the name of Gale Sayers, making it instantly one of the greatest drafts ever by a single team. Butkus charged out of the blocks like the bull he was. He recovered seven fumbles, picked off five passes, and wreaked so much havoc that he was a first-team All-Pro and Pro Bowl selection . . . as a rookie.

Over the next few years, his legend grew as bruised and battered opponents limped back to the locker room to try to explain what it was like to play against this particular Monster of the Midway. They would talk of his anger on the field, of his unrelenting drive, and of the lengths he would go to reach the ballcarrier—any lengths. Butkus combined a keen football mind able to predict plays before they happened with a take-no-prisoners style that would have been at home in the pre-facemask, leather-helmet days before the NFL was even born. The man simply loved to hit people.

Butkus also excelled at finding the football. When he retired, no one had ever recovered more opponents' fumbles than Butkus's total of 27. Though he, like any defensive player, longed for the end zone, he managed to return just one of those for a touchdown, and that was in his final season.

CAREER STATS

Yrs.	Sacks	Int.	FR
9	n/a	22	27

The arrival of that final season, 1973, was hastened by a serious knee injury suffered in 1970. Butkus's career was only nine seasons, the final three on a bum knee, and it included, much to his regret, no playoff appearances. But he left a legend that has not been lessened by time. Younger fans probably know him more for his many acting roles, as he has used that tough-guy image in movies, TV shows, and commercials—an old bear in winter, but still tough enough to take you.

6 POINTS

- Had 11 solo tackles in first NFL game
- Recovered seven fumbles in first NFL season
- Recorded only career safety in 1969
- Kicked successful PATs in each of 1971 and 1972 seasons
- Top college linebacker is honored with the Butkus Award
- Named to NFL's 75th Anniversary All-Time Team in 1994

"If I had a choice, I'd sooner go one-on-one with a grizzly bear."
— *Packers RB MacArthur Lane*

TOP 10 MOST FEARED TACKLERS

1 DICK BUTKUS

Butkus hit so hard that there are probably 70-year-old running backs out there who are still sore.

2 NIGHT TRAIN LANE

Named for a train, hits like a train. From his safety spot, Lane chugged right through ballcarriers.

3 LAWRENCE TAYLOR

His rep was as a speed rusher, but he was just as fierce in keeping running backs from getting downfield.

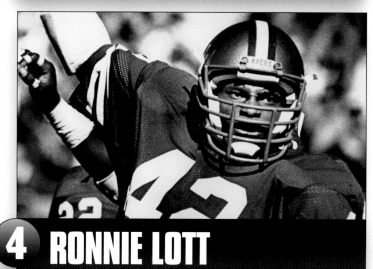

4 RONNIE LOTT

Lott had the speed and timing to play defensive back, but in his heart, he was a linebacker . . . and he hit like one.

5 HARDY BROWN

With the 49ers, Brown used his shoulders like fists; not well known today, he's remembered with bruises by opponents.

6 JACK TATUM

You don't earn a nickname like "The Assassin" without separating a few ballcarriers from the football.

7 RAY LEWIS

Lewis is an amazing combination of in-your-face toughness and line-spanning quickness.

8 JACK LAMBERT

Come across the middle or up the gut against Lambert, and he was more than happy to lower the Steel Curtain.

9 STEVE ATWATER

Like Lott, Atwater was a linebacker with a cornerback's number. He was especially good at attacking ballcarriers on the ends.

10 JOHN LYNCH

Lynch played only one way: all-out. He seemed to go out of his way to look for contact on just about every play.

No. 11 RONNIE LOTT

SAN FRANCISCO 49ERS
LOS ANGELES RAIDERS
NEW YORK JETS
KANSAS CITY CHIEFS

POSITION: CORNERBACK/SAFETY
YEARS: 1981–1994
HEIGHT: 6-0 WEIGHT: 205
SCHOOL: SOUTHERN CALIFORNIA
HALL OF FAME: 2000

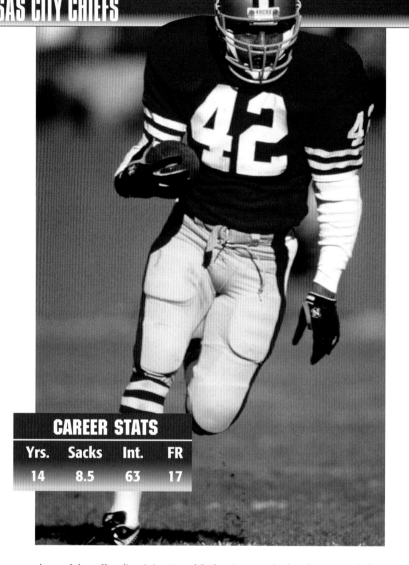

Just saying the name "Ronnie Lott" to wide receivers or running backs who played against him will probably elicit a cringe . . . almost two decades since the last time he put a hit on them. When Lott hit you, you stayed hit.

Regarded as one of the best and most fierce tacklers of all time, Lott was also one of the most versatile defensive backs in history. He earned Pro Bowl selections at cornerback, free safety, and strong safety, an unmatched record of skill at positions that are more different than many fans realize.

Lott began as a cornerback, using his speed and uncanny anticipation to track receivers downfield. Moving to strong safety in 1985, he got a chance to use his Dick Butkus–inspired tackling style to rack up five 100-tackle seasons. Switching to free safety, he became a field-spanning weapon, moving toward the ball and the play with almost-psychic perfection. Some players were better at each of the positions, but no one was better at all three than the former USC All-America.

In 1981, Lott got off to a fast start on his road to football immortality. He was only the second rookie ever to return three interceptions for touchdowns. He would have won the defensive rookie of the year award, if not for the presence of a certain Giants linebacker who went by the initials LT. Lott was part of a San Francisco 49ers defense that played a big part in the team winning its first NFL championship with Super Bowl XVI.

The 49ers won again three seasons later, as Lott led his defense in shutting down the Dolphins' Dan Marino–led passing attack in Super Bowl XIX.

Lott's reputation for toughness gained immeasurably in 1985. When his hand was smashed by an opponent's helmet, he ended up with a very damaged tip of his left pinky finger. Rather than miss games, including the playoffs, Lott told team doctors to just, well . . .

CAREER STATS			
Yrs.	Sacks	Int.	FR
14	8.5	63	17

chop of the offending joint. Tough? That just made the dictionary definition of the word.

Lott helped the Niners win two more Super Bowls in their dominance of the 1980s. He was named to the Pro Bowl in all but one of his 10 seasons with San Francisco. He got an additional Pro Bowl nod during his two seasons with the Raiders. He ended his career as a combination player-mentor with the New York Jets.

Lott left behind a legacy of ferocity, versatility, and toughness that has few, if any, equals.

6 POINTS

- All-America cornerback at USC
- Had nine interceptions in 20 career postseason games
- Led NFL in interceptions in 1986 and 1991
- Recovered 17 career fumbles
- 63 career interceptions are sixth-most all-time
- Named to NFL's 75th Anniversary All-Time Team in 1994

"He's devastating. He may dominate the secondary better than anyone I've seen."

— *Tom Landry*

No. 12 ANTHONY MUÑOZ

CINCINNATI BENGALS

POSITION: TACKLE
YEARS: 1980–1992
HEIGHT: 6-6 WEIGHT: 278
SCHOOL: SOUTHERN CALIFORNIA
HALL OF FAME: 1998

People had been playing some form of football for more than a century when Anthony Muñoz joined the NFL in 1980. You'd think that in all that time, players would have learned just about all there was to know about the simple art of blocking. Muñoz came along to show that there was an even better way to do it. Only one problem: He was the only man of his size who could accomplish most of the moves.

Though he came into the league as a bit of a gamble after three knee surgeries at USC and far fewer than the normal complement of collegiate games, Muñoz redefined offensive line play, especially the tackle position. Setting up with a wide, off-center stance that seemed to place him at a disadvantage, especially for a guy 6-6, he nonetheless had the speed and power to keep rushers from getting either inside or outside of him. With long arms and a wide base, he was a wall that defenders could neither scale nor topple. And you just didn't want to be the safety coming up to try to get at one of Muñoz's running backs; it's one thing to try to go over the wall . . . it's quite another to run smack into it.

A big part of Muñoz's success came from his intense conditioning. He was far ahead of his time in recognizing the importance of fitness for an offensive lineman. He had a weight room installed in his home, and made long-distance running a part of his regimen. Coaches couldn't believe that a guy his size would put in that much time in running shoes.

As the bedrock of Cincinnati's O-line from the day he arrived as a first-round draft pick, Muñoz helped the Bengals achieve their greatest successes, a pair of AFC championships (1981 and 1988), though Cincinnati lost Super Bowls XVI and XXIII to San Francisco. He was chosen for 11 straight Pro Bowls and won just about every award available for linemen.

CAREER STATS		
Yrs.	G	Pro Bowls
13	185	11

At the same time he was forging new paths for blockers, he was also acting as a sort of pioneer for Hispanic players. Few players with his heritage had reached such lofty NFL heights, and Muñoz took his job as a role model seriously, working with the league on outreach programs, and with kids.

In 1998, it was absolutely no surprise at all when Muñoz became the first Cincinnati Bengals player to be named to the Pro Football Hall of Fame. The man who redefined blocking had no roadblocks on the way to earning his bust in Canton.

"A better person than he was a player . . . Anthony is what heroes are supposed to look and act like."

— *Sam Wyche*

No. 13 JOE GREENE

PITTSBURGH STEELERS

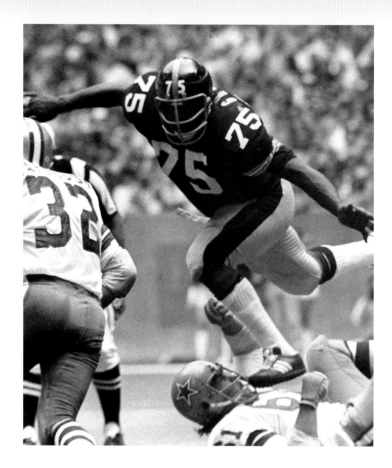

POSITION: DEFENSIVE TACKLE
YEARS: 1969–1981
HEIGHT: 6-4 WEIGHT: 275
SCHOOL: NORTH TEXAS
HALL OF FAME: 1987

I n 1969, everything changed for the Steelers, though no one really knew it at the time. They brought in a new coach, Chuck Noll. And Noll made his first draft pick a defensive lineman from North Texas State named Joe Greene. Most fans' reaction: Joe who?

Very soon, everyone knew the player who took his famous nickname, Mean Joe Greene, from his college's nickname—the Mean Green. An All-Pro and Pro Bowl selection as a rookie and winner of the AP defensive rookie of the year award, Greene was the foundation on which Noll built a defense that would carry the Steelers to four Super Bowl triumphs.

By 1974, the Greene-led Steel Curtain had turned Pittsburgh into the AFC champs. In Super Bowl IX, Greene again led the way, making an interception and recovering a fumble as the Steelers won their first title with a 16–6 throttling of the Vikings.

The hits just kept on coming, as Pittsburgh won its four titles in six seasons. Greene was the AP NFL defensive player of the year in 1972 and 1974 and earned four more first-team All-Pro selections. Greene's greatest strengths were in attacking the quarterback, but he was equally tough on ballcarriers.

Greene's and the Steelers' success, and the emergence of the NFL and the Super Bowl as a truly huge national media phenomenon, helped him take part in one of the most memorable TV commercials ever. In 1979, after Pittsburgh had established itself as a dynasty and Greene had a nickname-induced reputation, he filmed a spot for Coca-Cola that has been seen millions of times since and parodied almost as much. In the commercial, a gruff, grimy Greene is limping down the tunnel after a tough game. A kid asks, "You need any help?" Then he offers the player a Coke. The granite cracks a little, Greene relents,

CAREER STATS			
Yrs.	Sacks	Int.	FR
13	n/a	1	16

chugs a Coke, and then smiles and tosses the kid his jersey. "Wow," the kid says. "Thanks, Mean Joe."

Overnight, Greene wasn't so mean anymore. Between the nickname and the commercial, Greene was elevated into more than just a part of a ferocious, winning defense—he became an icon. You don't get that status just for being telegenic, however. Greene earned his real football chops on the field. Look around in the top 20 of this NFL Top 100 . . . only Reggie White appears before Greene among defensive linemen. Mean? That's not mean, that's marvelous.

"Joe Greene is the most important player in the history of the Pittsburgh Steelers."

— *Dennis Miller*

No. 14 SAMMY BAUGH

WASHINGTON REDSKINS

POSITION: QUARTERBACK/PUNTER/SAFETY
YEARS: 1937–1952
HEIGHT: 6-2 **WEIGHT:** 180
SCHOOL: TEXAS CHRISTIAN
HALL OF FAME: 1963

CAREER STATS				
Yrs.	W-L	Yds.	TD	Rating
16	n/a	21,886	187	72.2

There was nothing that Sammy Baugh could not do on a football field . . . and almost nothing that anyone could do better. For all-around greatness as a player, no one can match Baugh's quadruple-threat of skills.

—He led the NFL in passing six times, an unsurpassed mark.

—Baugh's 1940 average of 51.4 yards per punt is still the highest single-season mark . . . ever. Oakland's Shane Lechler came within an eyelash of topping that in 2009—69 years after Baugh's big year. And Baugh is the only man to lead the league in punting four consecutive seasons.

—He led the NFL in interceptions in 1943 with 11, part of his career total of 31 picks.

—Just for fun, he also ran for nine touchdowns and returned punts once in a while.

The capper to this display of "mad skills"—a phrase that would have made the rawboned Texan's face probably get a funny look—was the 1943 season in which he was Tom Brady, Charles Woodson, and Shane Lechler all rolled into one. That year, Baugh became the first player (and we can safely add "only" and mean it) to lead the NFL in passing, punting, *and* interceptions.

Baugh's greatest contributions, however, came as a passer. When he started his career in 1937 after a two-time All-America college career at TCU, passing was just starting to come into vogue, but it had yet to become a truly powerful offensive weapon. "Slingin' Sammy" changed all that. Firing passes long and short, Baugh singlehandedly carried the NFL out of the dust and into the air. The keys were his accuracy (he led the NFL in completion percentage nine times and his 70.33 mark in 1945 is still the third-best ever) and attitude—he'd throw any pass anywhere, especially when opposing teams were not expecting it. He wasn't afraid to put it up, either—he also led the NFL three times in throwing interceptions.

He announced his presence early, going 11-for-16 in his first game and capping off his rookie year by throwing for three touchdowns in the Redskins' first NFL championship.

In 1940, Baugh and the Redskins were on the receiving end of the worst pasting in NFL history: a 73–0 loss to the Bears in the NFL Championship Game. Two years later, Baugh got his revenge, beating the Bears for the title 14–6. In 1944, the Redskins finally switched to the T-formation. That's right, fans: up to this point, Baugh had set all those records and won all those passing titles out of a single-wing formation designed to exploit the run. Once he got the hang of the T, Baugh got even better, leading the NFL in attempts, completions, and passing yards in 1947 and 1948.

In Sammy Baugh, you have the complete package of NFL skills on offense and defense. You have a player who set the standard for greatness as a pro passer. And you have a player whose all-around skills will probably never be seen again.

- Earned nickname as baseball player for great arm
- First defensive player to set record of four interceptions in one game (1943)
- 45.1 yards per punt career average is fifth all-time
- Had career-high six TD passes in 1947 game
- Starred in Western movie "King of the Texas Rangers"
- Member of inaugural class of Pro Football Hall of Fame

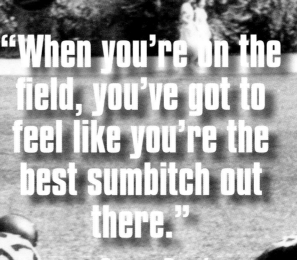

"When you're on the field, you've got to feel like you're the best sumbitch out there."

— *Sammy Baugh*

DEACON JONES

LOS ANGELES RAMS
SAN DIEGO CHARGERS
WASHINGTON REDSKINS

POSITION: **DEFENSIVE END**
YEARS: **1961–1974**
HEIGHT: **6-5** WEIGHT: **272**
SCHOOL: **SOUTH CAROLINA STATE/MISSISSIPPI VOC.**
HALL OF FAME: **1980**

Deacon Jones would probably hate to play in the NFL today. For very appropriate safety reasons, some of the painful ferocity of the way Jones liked to play defensive end has been legislated out of the game. After all, this was a player whose favorite mode of attacking the offensive linemen tasked with stopping him was a solid whack to the helmet—the head slap. And after a while, even if he didn't headslap you, just the thought of getting your bell rung would put you enough off stride that Jones would be by you and on the way to the QB.

When Jones played in the NFL, sacks were not counted as an official statistic, so there's no way to know where exactly he ranks on the all-time list. But without Jones, we might not have a name for what that list counts: He invented the word "sack" to describe tackling the quarterback for a loss. One unofficial tally by the Rams gave him 26 sacks in 1967 . . . which would be an all-time single-season record, if it counted.

Jones had sacks on his mind but a chip on his shoulder when he started in the NFL in 1961. He had been overlooked by only the most zealous of scouts during his brief college career (and those Rams scouts had only seen him while visiting Mississippi to watch one of Jones's teammates). So when he went in the 14th round, an African-American from the segregated South used to a system of life that kept him down, the NFL gave him freedom to be himself. He took the draft slight, the frustrations of a life apart, and his small-college status as fuel and ignited one of the best defensive careers in NFL history.

Teaming with fellow Hall of Famer Merlin Olsen and other stars, Jones was part of the Fearsome Foursome for the Rams. In 1972, he was traded to the Chargers and continued his sack-happy ways, making the AFC Pro Bowl team. For his final season in 1974, he played one

CAREER STATS

Yrs.	Sacks	Int.	FR
16	n/a	2	15

year under George Allen at Washington. Allen had been his Rams coach from 1966–1970 and a man who, according to writer Jennifer Allen, George's daughter, was the first white man to give Jones a chance to lead.

Judging from the way that Jones played, it was either lead, follow, or get out of the way. Jones led; his defensive teammates followed; and opponents simply tried to get out of the way. Most of the time, they couldn't.

- Played one year at South Carolina State
- Gave himself nickname, saying there were too many David Joneses
- Kicked an extra point in final regular season game of career (1974)
- First-team All-Pro from 1965 to 1969
- Chosen NFL defensive player of the year by AP, 1967 and 1962
- Named to NFL's 75th Anniversary All-Time Team in 1994

"I just take all the offensive players and put them in a bag and get a baseball bat and beat on the bag."

— Deacon Jones

No. 16 OTTO GRAHAM
CLEVELAND BROWNS

POSITION: QUARTERBACK
YEARS: 1946–1955
HEIGHT: 6-1 WEIGHT: 196
SCHOOL: NORTHWESTERN
HALL OF FAME: 1965

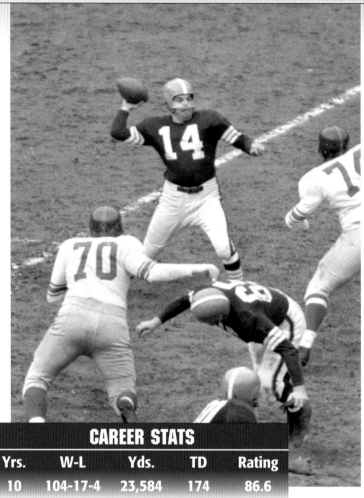

CAREER STATS				
Yrs.	W-L	Yds.	TD	Rating
10	104-17-4	23,584	174	86.6

His record is almost unbelievable. It's hard to calculate the worth of a player who achieved today what Otto Graham did in his mid-century career. If a player today did what Graham did, his team would probably have to just give him the stadium.

Graham played 10 seasons as the starting quarterback for the Cleveland Browns. In every one of those 10 seasons, he led his team into his league's championship game. No one has even come close to that record.

The first four of those came when Cleveland was part of the All-America Football Conference. Or should we say "all" of the AAFC? That short-lived league had only one champion in its four seasons: the Browns, led by Graham and legendary coach Paul Brown. In 1950, the NFL absorbed the most stable AAFC teams, including the Browns. Most experts figured that the new kids would wilt beneath the power of the older league. But in the Browns' first game in their new league, they beat the defending NFL-champion Philadelphia Eagles. At the end of that first season, Graham carried the Browns to their first NFL title and fifth championship in a row overall. The scene would repeat itself, in part, for five more seasons. Talk about a dynasty: The Browns would play for the championship six times in their first six NFL seasons, and win three of those games.

Such success was not a given for Graham, who had not planned to play even college football, let alone pro. Basketball was his sport (along with enough musical talent that he considered that career, too). However, after being discovered while playing intramural football, he became a star at Northwestern. Paul Brown made Graham the linchpin of his new AAFC team in 1946, and together they brought the T-formation three more steps forward. An accurate passer, Graham was also a nimble runner and fiery leader.

After they ran the table in the AAFC and won the NFL crown in 1950, the Browns lost three straight NFL Championship Games. Just making the final game wasn't enough, however, and they stormed back to the 1954 game. Graham made sure of victory in a big way, passing for three touchdowns and rushing for three more. Cleveland won the game 56–10 and Graham retired.

Temporarily.

Paul Brown called in desperation before the 1955 season, and Graham came back for one more fling. No surprise here that he led the team to another NFL title, capping off his amazing career by passing for two scores and running for two more in his final game, a 38–14 win over the Rams.

He played before the big money, before the national TV, before the glitz and glamour . . . but all these years later, no one has topped what he did: 10 title games in 10 years.

- Studied French horn at Northwestern
- Was also defensive back and punt returner in AAFC
- Nickname: Automatic Otto
- Led league in passing yards five times
- Led league in touchdown passes three times
- Also played pro basketball for Rochester Royals

"The test of a quarterback is where his team finishes. By that standard, Otto Graham was the best."

— *Paul Brown*

No. 17 BARRY SANDERS

DETROIT LIONS

POSITION: RUNNING BACK
YEARS: 1989–1998
HEIGHT: 5-8 WEIGHT: 203
SCHOOL: OKLAHOMA STATE
HALL OF FAME: 2004

CAREER STATS				
Yrs.	Att.	Yds.	Yds./Carry	Rush TDs
10	3,062	15,269	5.0	99

Time to dip into another sport to come up with a comparison for how Barry Sanders ran the football. "The only way to catch a knuckleball," said baseball legend Casey Stengel, "is to wait for it to stop rolling and then pick it up." Barry Sanders was a human knuckleball.

With moves that put contortionists to shame and bursts of speed that left defenders grasping air, Sanders put on show after show of amazing football dexterity . . . with his feet.

In a decade of rushing brilliance—a career that ended far too early for the liking of Lions fans—Sanders created almost a century's worth of highlights. His ability to make tacklers miss and his creativity in twisting, spinning, and avoiding turned him into the player fans loved to watch and defensive coordinators hoped to avoid.

He was already a record-setting runner after a sterling career at Oklahoma State that included the 1988 Heisman Trophy. As a rookie with the Lions in 1989, he set a team record with 1,470 yards (and the Lions have been around since 1930!). He just missed the NFL rushing title that year, but he fixed that in 1990 with a league-leading 1,304 yards. He also led the NFL in touchdowns that year with 16. His numbers over the next few seasons were just eye-popping. Sanders was the first back to record 1,000-yard seasons in his first 10 seasons. The 1990 title was the first of four league rushing titles he earned.

Sanders managed to rack up all these yards despite playing for a Lions team that didn't have much else to surround him, but with the addition of Sanders made the playoffs five times in his career. He also did it at a size (5-8) considered a bit puny by NFL standards. But it gave him a lower center of gravity that actually made the moves created by his powerful legs more achievable.

In 1997, he had the most amazing of his many amazing seasons. He became the third player ever to top 2,000 yards, and his final total of 2,053 is the third highest all-time (through 2010). He topped 1,400 yards in 1998, and the only thing ahead of him looked to be the all-time rushing record then held by Walter Payton.

But Sanders pulled another fast one, going a different way than everyone expected him to go: At the age of 30, he retired from football.

His fans were shocked. His teammates were hurt, but understood. His opponents were positively giddy.

Though he left with perhaps more gas in the tank, Sanders had taken a whole lot of footballs on one terrific ride.

- Gained 2,628 yards in junior-year Heisman campaign
- 10 yards short of NFL rushing title as rookie in 1989
- Six seasons with 11-plus rushing TDs
- 2,358 yards from scrimmage in 1997 is fifth-best ever
- First runner with five 1,500-yard seasons
- Named NFL MVP for 1997

"By the time you get to where Barry is, he's not there anymore."

— *Jerry Ball*

No. 18 RAY LEWIS

BALTIMORE RAVENS

POSITION: LINEBACKER
YEARS: 1996–
HEIGHT: 6-1 WEIGHT: 245
SCHOOL: MIAMI (FL)

A ll we have here to tell the story of Ray Lewis is words and pictures. They'll give you a sense of him as a player and as a person, but he's one player who has to be seen to be truly appreciated. We can tell you about his run-stuffing tackles, about his sideline-to-sideline chases of running backs, about his "don't come across the middle" hits on tight ends and receivers. We can recount his awards, stats, and honors. But until you've been in the huddle with him, until you've been led by him on and off the field, until you've felt that heartbeat and intensity that Ravens players and fans have enjoyed since 1996, you can't really know what we're talking about.

Lewis was an All-America at Miami and ended up as a first-round draft pick of the Ravens, who were also making their NFL debut. Lewis instantly became the centerpiece of a defense that would define the franchise for the next decade-plus. Making the first of his 12 Pro Bowls (so far) as a rookie, Lewis was the NFL's leading tackler by 1997.

He quickly established himself as the most feared tackler in the game, combining intensity and ferocity with picture-perfect technique. He was almost as good dropping into coverage, too, with at least one interception in each of his first eight seasons.

In 2000, he brought all his skills together at their highest peak, and the Ravens had an offense that was good enough to win games, too. Baltimore won the AFC championship with a stunning defensive playoff run: they allowed a combined 16 points in three postseason games to earn a place in Super Bowl XXXV. The Lewis-led D put on a show for the ages in that game against the Giants. The only score for New York that day came on a kickoff return; otherwise, nothing. Lewis was named the MVP of the game, only the sixth time a defender won the honor, and he won it as much for leadership as for his stats.

CAREER STATS			
Yrs.	Sacks	Int.	FR
15	38.5	30	19

He was named the NFL defensive player of the year a second time in 2003 as he continued to set the tone for one of the league's best defenses. Even after 14 seasons in the NFL, he was earning first-team All-Pro honors in 2009.

After all this, Lewis joins a pantheon of the greatest ever at his position: Schmidt, Butkus, Nitschke, Singletary, Lewis. He's right in there and some experts put him atop that list. We certainly wouldn't argue the point with him if we had a football in our hands.

6 POINTS

- Selected to Pro Bowl every healthy season since rookie year
- Scored three TDs on interception returns
- Seven-time first-team All-Pro
- Eight seasons with 100-plus tackles
- Ravens in top five of NFL defenses eight times since 1999
- Recovered 19 fumbles and registered 38.5 sacks

"Give us 10 points and the game is over. That's not boasting. If you give us 10 points, game over. You go down against our defense, you're in a whole lot of trouble."

— *Lewis to the Ravens' offense before Super Bowl XXXV*

No. 19 BRONKO NAGURSKI

CHICAGO BEARS

POSITION: FULLBACK
YEARS: 1930–1937, 1943
HEIGHT: 6-2 WEIGHT: 226
SCHOOL: MINNESOTA
HALL OF FAME: 1963

id any player ever have a greater football name than Bronko Nagurski? Did any player ever combine all-pro skills on both offense and defense better than Bronko Nagurski? The answer to both is no. With a name that sounded like one of his teeth-rattling plunges into the line, Nagurski was the mold from which generations of NFL running backs were cut. Big, strong, and focused, he helped the Chicago Bears win three NFL championships. His stats are far from eye-popping when compared to today's computer-popping totals, but for his time, there was no one better.

Nagurski started his assault on America's football consciousness as a two-way star at the University of Minnesota. With the Golden Gophers (a pretty great name itself), he was an All-America as a fullback and as a defensive tackle, the first player ever to earn that dual honor. Joining the Bears in 1930, he was the thunder to Red Grange's lightning. That's right, two of the NFL's most illustrious early heroes shared the backfield in Chicago.

In 1932, a tie in the final standings led to an additional regular-season game to determine the NFL champion. Before that point, the winner of the league was simply the team with the best record. That game, against the Portsmouth Spartans, who later became the Detroit Lions, turned not on Nagurski's pounding running, but on a creative play of which he was the master: the jump pass. As he took the ball behind the line and thundered toward the defense—which naturally swarmed to try to stop him—Nagurski would stop and jump straight up. From the top of his jump, he would sling a pass. In the 1932 game, it went to Grange for the game's only touchdown.

The next year, the NFL took the thrill of that extra game and made it official: starting in 1933, the NFL champion was the team that won

CAREER STATS				
Yrs.	Att.	Yds.	Yds./Carry	Rush TDs
9	633	2,778	4.4	25

the annual championship game. How fitting that Nagurski threw for two more touchdowns as the Bears beat the Giants, 23–21. In 1934, it was behind the power of Nagurski's blocking (how fierce could he be when he didn't have to protect the football?) that Beattie Feathers of Chicago, taking over after Grange, became the first back to reach 1,000 rushing yards in a season.

- Born in Canada; real name was Bronislaw
- Led NFL with four rushing TDs in 1932
- Ranked in top eight in yards per carry five times
- Following 1932 playoff game, rules were changed to increase passing
- Five-time All-Pro
- Member of inaugural class of Pro Football Hall of Fame

> "My biggest thrill in football was the day Bronko Nagurski announced his retirement."
>
> — *Battered defender Clark Hinkle*

Did any NFL player ever have a more fitting post-football career? Nagurski retired in 1938 to become a professional wrestler, using his massive strength and famous name to become a star in another sport. Yet in 1943, with the Bears depleted by the war, the then-35-year-old came back to the gridiron. Taking over at fullback, he led the Bears to yet another NFL title.

No. 20 BRETT FAVRE

- ATLANTA FALCONS
- GREEN BAY PACKERS
- NEW YORK JETS
- MINNESOTA VIKINGS

POSITION: QUARTERBACK
YEARS: 1991–2010
HEIGHT: 6-2 **WEIGHT:** 225
SCHOOL: SOUTHERN MISSISSIPPI

Quarterback Brett Favre completed more passes in more attempts for more yards and more touchdowns than anyone else in NFL history—and all by a wide margin. (Arguably, he also threw more interceptions and retired and un-retired more often than anyone else.) But for all of his remarkable statistics, the one that stands out the most is this: He made 297 consecutive starts from early in the 1992 season until late in the 2010 season. That's an NFL record for longevity and durability that may never be matched.

Most of Favre's starts came for the Green Bay Packers, for whom he played from 1992 to 2007, a 16-year tenure highlighted by a Super Bowl victory in the 1996 season. Favre actually had been drafted by Atlanta in the second round in 1991, but the Falcons shipped him to Green Bay in exchange for a first-round draft pick. That was a steep price for a player who did not complete a pass in his rookie season, but Packers general manager Ron Wolf knew what he was getting. (While with the Jets a year earlier, Wolf had wanted to draft Favre but wound up with Browning Nagle instead when the Falcons took the former Southern Mississippi star.)

Favre began his Packers career as a backup to Don Majkowski, and then came off the bench after Majkowski was injured early in the third game of the 1992 season, against Cincinnati. Favre passed for the winning touchdown in the final seconds against the Bengals and never relinquished his hold on the quarterback job.

Favre ended up playing 20 NFL seasons. He was a throwback to a different era, a time long before the Internet age, when quarterbacks improvised plays on rock-hard dirt fields and rarely came out of games. He kept his starting streak going by playing through a separated shoulder, a sprained ankle, a broken thumb, and various bumps and bruises. He had a gunslinger mentality and a supreme confidence that not only contributed to his record-setting interception

CAREER STATS				
Yrs.	W-L	Yds.	TD	Rating
20	181-104	71,838	508	86.0

total, but also helped him rally against seemingly impossible odds. In fact, his comeback against the Bengals in 1992 was the first of 40 victories that he engineered in Green Bay with the Packers trailing or tied in the fourth quarter or overtime.

Favre finally called it quits at the close of the 2007 season after 253 consecutive starts for the Packers. But when he decided during training camp in 2008 that he wanted to return, relations with the club became strained and he eventually leveraged a trade to the Jets. After one season in New York, he retired again, only to return with Minnesota in 2009.

- Was on the receiving end of his own deflected pass for his first career completion
- Equaled quarterback Bart Starr's record of 16 seasons in a Packers uniform
- In 2007, surpassed John Elway for most career wins as an NFL starting quarterback
- Record NFL career passing totals include 71,838 yards and 508 touchdowns
- While with the Jets in 2008, passed for six touchdowns in a game against the Cardinals
- First player to earn three NFL MVP awards from the AP

Though Favre may have tainted his legacy with his vacillations over retirement, he also had one of his best seasons in 2009, the year he turned 40. That season, he compiled a career-best passer rating of 107.2, earned his 11th Pro Bowl selection, and led the Vikings to 12 regular season victories and a berth in the NFC title game. The 2010 season did not go as well, and, late in the year, a shoulder injury put an end to his starting streak. At the end of the year, he retired for good. (We think!)

TOP 10 MOST ELUSIVE RUNNERS

1 BARRY SANDERS
Imagine using chopsticks to catch mercury sliding on a glass plate. That's the experience of trying to tackle Sanders.

2 GALE SAYERS
Breakaway speed with ankle-breaking moves, Sayers had it all—just too bad he only had it for four-plus seasons.

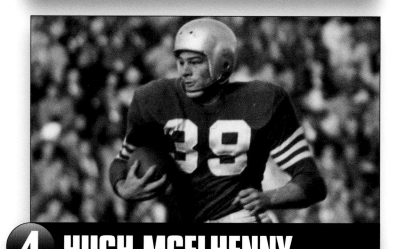

3 MARSHALL FAULK

Faulk was like a stealth Sanders—it seemed like you had him bang to rights and then, suddenly, he was past you.

4 HUGH MCELHENNY
The term swivel-hips was perfect for the man they called "The King," who ruled the Niners in the 1950s.

5 BOBBY MITCHELL

Mitchell excelled in the open field, often leaving tacklers grasping nothing but air as he headed for the end zone.

6 RED GRANGE

In a time in which force and power was the norm, Grange's moves created a new way to play the game.

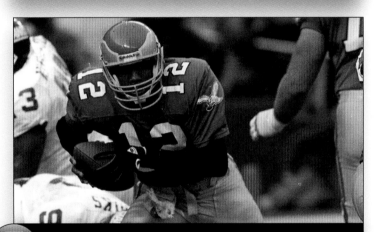

7 RANDALL CUNNINGHAM

How'd a quarterback get in here? A superb all-around athlete, Cunningham never let his height stop him from being elusive.

8 JOE WASHINGTON

One of the quintessential "scatbacks," Washington was 5-10, but he was so hard to catch, he actually "played" smaller.

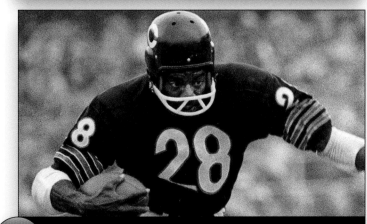

9 DICKIE POST

Among the words opponents used to describe Post: crab, gnat, mouse, hare. Good luck trying to catch any of those!

10 WILLIE GALIMORE

Sprinters' speed and the moves of a snake on two legs, Galimore's running was like his too-short life: a blur.

No.  21 TOM BRADY

NEW ENGLAND PATRIOTS

POSITION: QUARTERBACK
YEARS: 2000–
HEIGHT: 6-4 WEIGHT: 225
SCHOOL: MICHIGAN

		CAREER STATS		
Yrs.	**W-L**	**Yds.**	**TD**	**Rating**
11	97-30	34,744	261	95.2

Tom Brady was just a youngster in the stands when quarterback Joe Montana launched the San Francisco 49ers' dynasty of the 1980s. It was Montana's winning touchdown drive late in the fourth quarter that cinched the 1981 NFC title game against the Dallas Cowboys. Two decades later, Brady was the quarterback who launched the New England Patriots' dynasty of the 2000s, with the winning field goal drive late in the fourth quarter of Super Bowl XXXVI against the St. Louis Rams.

Like Montana, Brady was a seemingly unlikely hero who dropped in the NFL Draft because of questions over his physical skills. But what scouts could not measure in either of those stars were the leadership abilities and other intangibles that made them among the best ever to play quarterback in the NFL.

Brady, in fact, lasted until the 199th overall pick of the 2000 draft when the Patriots, who already had veteran Drew Bledsoe behind center, tabbed him in the sixth round. After playing little as a rookie, Brady stepped into the lineup when Bledsoe was injured early in the 2001 season. But even after the veteran was ready to return, head coach Bill Belichick saw what he had in his second-year quarterback, and he stayed with the youngster. New England posted six consecutive victories down the stretch and won the AFC East.

In the postseason, Brady's legend was born. First, he directed the game-tying field goal drive in the fourth quarter and the game-winning field goal drive in overtime of a divisional-playoff victory over the Raiders in a driving snowstorm. Then came the winning march with no timeouts left late in the Super Bowl against the Rams.

That was the first of three Super Bowl championships in a four-season span for the Patriots (a feat matched only by the Dallas Cowboys in the 1990s). Then, with Brady passing for an NFL-record 50 touchdowns and directing the highest-scoring offense in NFL history,

the 2007 Patriots became the first team in the 16-game era to win every regular season game. Only a last-minute upset loss to the New York Giants in Super Bowl XLII kept New England from completing a perfect season.

Brady was the Associated Press's NFL MVP that year, as well as in 2010, when he passed for 36 touchdowns against only four interceptions. Included in that was a record streak of 339 straight pass attempts without an interception. The Patriots went 14–2 that year but again were upset in the postseason, this time by the New York Jets in the divisional round.

Still, Brady and Belichick remained the constants that helped make the Patriots the NFL's unofficial Team of the 2000s. Just like with Montana and head coach Bill Walsh in San Francisco in the 1980s, neither man may have been as successful without the other. That's a chicken-egg question that can never be answered. One thing is for certain, though: Both Brady and Belichick eventually will be inducted into the Pro Football Hall of Fame.

6 POINTS

- Quarterbacked Michigan to 10 victories in his senior season in 1999
- Won 100 regular season games faster than any other NFL quarterback (131 starts)
- Passed for three or more TDs in 10 games in a row in 2007
- MVP of Patriots' wins in Super Bowl XXXVI and XXXVIII
- Missed almost all of 2008 season after injuring his knee
- Married to Brazilian supermodel Gisele Bündchen

GALE SAYERS

CHICAGO BEARS

POSITION: RUNNING BACK
YEARS: 1965–1971
HEIGHT: 6-0 WEIGHT: 198
SCHOOL: KANSAS
HALL OF FAME: 1977

E ven before he played in the pros, running back Gale Sayers was nicknamed the "Kansas Comet." But he was more like a fireball that burned brightly in the NFL skies, and then disappeared quickly—too quickly for Chicago Bears fans.

The Bears selected Sayers with the fourth overall pick of the 1965 NFL Draft, right after they chose linebacker Dick Butkus at number three. While Butkus solidified the defense, Sayers gave Chicago an electrifying presence on offense and as a return man on special teams. He combined lightning speed with a dazzling array of moves and keen football instincts to a degree unmatched in the 40 years since his retirement. (Perhaps only Barry Sanders, Detroit's Pro Football Hall of Fame running back, has come close.)

In Sayers's second NFL game, he raced 18 yards for a touchdown against the Los Angeles Rams. The next week, he ran for a touchdown and caught a touchdown pass against the Packers. By season's end, Sayers had scored 22 touchdowns—a record for NFL rookies. Six of those scores came in one memorable performance against the 49ers: Only two players before Sayers ever scored six touchdowns in a single game, and no one has since.

Sayers led the NFL in rushing in 1966, and topped the league in combined net yards (rushing, receiving, and returns) in each of his first three years. Then, late in the 1968 season, he suffered a serious knee injury. Though he came back to lead the league in rushing again in 1969, he no longer was the same player. More injuries followed, and by 1971 he was forced to retire after only seven NFL seasons.

6 POINTS

- At 34 in 1977, was youngest player inducted into the Pro Football Hall of Fame
- Returned six kickoffs and two punts for TDs in his career
- Holds NFL record with career average of 30.6 yards per kickoff return
- One of the best open-field runners in NFL history
- Big day against the 49ers in 1965 included 80-yard catch, 50-yard run, and 85-yard punt return
- Offensive Player of the Game in three of four Pro Bowls

JOHN ELWAY No. 23

DENVER BRONCOS

POSITION: QUARTERBACK
YEARS: 1983–1998
HEIGHT: 6-3 WEIGHT: 215
SCHOOL: STANFORD
HALL OF FAME: 2004

John Elway can claim something that no other player in the history of the NFL can: He was the Super Bowl's most valuable player in the final game of his career. The Denver Broncos' strong-armed quarterback hoisted the Pete Rozelle Trophy as the MVP after leading his team to a 34–19 victory over the Atlanta Falcons in Super Bowl XXXIII to cap the 1998 season. It was a storybook ending to a storybook career.

Elway made a habit of rallying his teams from the brink of defeat. His most famous comeback was the "The Drive," a 98-yard march to tie the 1986 AFC title game at Cleveland, a contest Denver won in overtime. Yet, for a long time, it seemed as if he was fated to fall short of the pinnacle of his profession. He routinely made the Pro Bowl (nine times in his 16 seasons) and passed for more than 3,000 yards (12 times) while carrying the Broncos on his back to the playoffs. But once the team reached the postseason, the lack of a running game doomed Denver. Then the Broncos paired Elway with power runner Terrell Davis in the mid-1990s, and Denver's newfound balance helped catapult the team to its first Super Bowl victory in the 1997 season (game XXXII against Green Bay). Elway pondered retirement after that game but came back and passed for 336 yards in Denver's victory over Atlanta in game XXXIII.

The lasting image from that Super Bowl is Elway grinning from ear to ear at one of his offensive linemen after running for a touchdown in the fourth quarter. Earlier in his career, Elway had been one of the NFL's best scramblers, but at 38 he no longer ran much. On this play, though, he took off from three yards out and dove into the end zone for the touchdown that put an exclamation point on a Hall-of-Fame career.

6 POINTS

- Played minor-league baseball in Yankees' organization
- Drafted No. 1 overall in 1983 by the Colts
- Led Denver to 46 game-winning drives in the fourth quarter or overtime
- Only NFL player to pass for 3,000 yards and rush for 200 yards seven seasons in a row
- Caught 23-yard TD pass in 1986 game against the Raiders
- Named NFL MVP for 1987

No. 24 JOHN HANNAH

NEW ENGLAND PATRIOTS

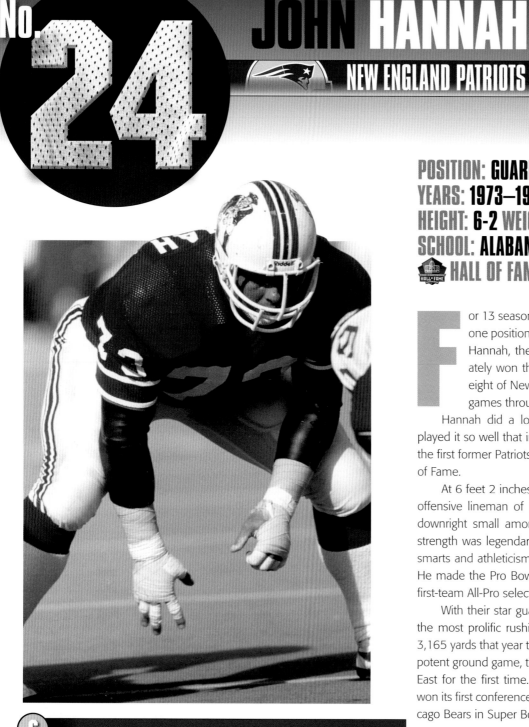

POSITION: GUARD
YEARS: 1973–1985
HEIGHT: 6-2 WEIGHT: 265
SCHOOL: ALABAMA
HALL OF FAME: 1991

For 13 seasons beginning in 1973, Patriots head coaches had one position they didn't have to worry about: left guard. John Hannah, the club's first-round draft pick that year, immediately won the starting job and was in the lineup for all but eight of New England's 190 regular season and postseason games through Super Bowl XX in the 1985 season.

Hannah did a lot more than just fill the position, though. He played it so well that in 1991, in his first year of eligibility, he became the first former Patriots player to be inducted into the Pro Football Hall of Fame.

At 6 feet 2 inches and 265 pounds, Hannah was not the biggest offensive lineman of his era (and he would have been considered downright small among the supersized blockers of today). But his strength was legendary, and he combined that strength with football smarts and athleticism that made him the premier guard of his time. He made the Pro Bowl after nine of his final 10 seasons, and was a first-team All-Pro selection seven times.

With their star guard leading the way, the 1978 Patriots featured the most prolific rushing attack in NFL history. New England ran for 3,165 yards that year to set a league single-season record. Behind that potent ground game, the Patriots posted 11 victories and won the AFC East for the first time. In 1985, Hannah's last season, New England won its first conference championship. Hannah started against the Chicago Bears in Super Bowl XX in the final game of his career.

6 POINTS

- Also starred in wrestling and in track and field while in college at Alabama
- NFL Players Association's Offensive Lineman of the Year each season from 1978 to 1981
- Named to NFL's All-Decade Team of both 1970s and 1980s
- Named Patriots' "Player of the Century" in fan voting (2000)
- Jersey number 73 officially has been retired by New England
- Brother Charley Hannah played in the NFL (1977–88)

DAN MARINO No. 25

MIAMI DOLPHINS

POSITION: QUARTERBACK
YEARS: 1983–1999
HEIGHT: 6-4 WEIGHT: 224
SCHOOL: PITTSBURGH
HALL OF FAME: 2005

W e all know the old saying about hindsight being 20/20. Even still, it seems inexplicable today that 26 teams passed on Dan Marino in the first round of the 1983 NFL Draft before the Miami Dolphins selected him. Sure, the Denver Broncos can't complain: They wound up with John Elway after making a trade with the Baltimore Colts, who selected him with the top overall pick that year. And the Buffalo Bills got Jim Kelly, although he didn't join the team until 1986, after a stint in the USFL. But that first-round draft class included six quarterbacks—Todd Blackledge, Tony Eason, and Ken O'Brien all went before Marino, too—not to mention a handful of forgettable names at other positions.

Seventeen seasons later, Marino retired as the NFL's most prolific passer. (Brett Favre has since surpassed his marks.) That was quite an achievement considering that Miami always was a run-first team before Marino's arrival. But legendary coach Don Shula recognized the gem he had in his rookie signal caller, and the Dolphins transformed overnight into a passing team.

Marino, whose greatest asset was a lightning-quick release, started nine games in his rookie season and made the Pro Bowl. The next year, while leading Miami to the AFC championship (the Dolphins lost to the 49ers in Super Bowl XIX), he became the first NFL quarterback to pass for 5,000 yards in a season, and his 48 touchdowns set another record that stood 20 years. He was the first quarterback to pass for 50,000 yards, and first to reach 60,000 yards. His final tally: 61,361 yards, 420 touchdowns, and 26 regretful NFL teams.

6 POINTS

- **Earned nine Pro Bowl selections**
- **Still holds the NFL single-season record of 5,084 passing yards (1984)**
- **His uniform No. 13 officially retired by the Dolphins**
- **Played more games (242) than anyone in Miami's history**
- **Passed for 400 or more yards in a game a record 13 times**
- **Had a string of 30 consecutive games with a touchdown pass (1985–87)**

No. 26 BOB LILLY

DALLAS COWBOYS

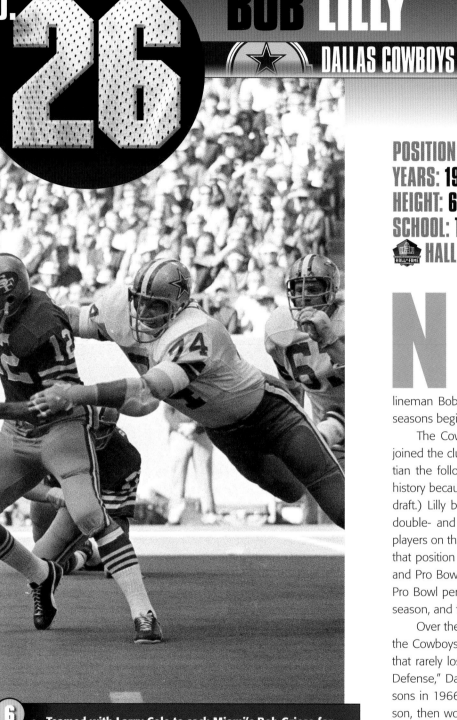

POSITION: DEFENSIVE LINE
YEARS: 1961–1974
HEIGHT: 6-5 WEIGHT: 260
SCHOOL: TEXAS CHRISTIAN
HALL OF FAME: 1980

Not many NFL franchises can boast the star power of the Dallas Cowboys. Their long history of winning teams, regular appearances on the national stage, and a penchant for the dramatic have made Dallas's top players mythic figures. But to the team's legion of fans across the country, there's only one "Mr. Cowboy." That's defensive lineman Bob Lilly, who was the cornerstone of the franchise for 14 seasons beginning with the club's formative years.

The Cowboys were an NFL expansion team in 1960, and Lilly joined the club as a first-round draft choice out of nearby Texas Christian the following season. (Trivia item: He was the first pick in club history because the franchise was formed too late to join in the 1960 draft.) Lilly began his career as a defensive end, and—though often double- and even triple-teamed by opponents who had few other players on the Dallas defense to worry about—he was good enough at that position to earn league rookie of the year notice his first season and Pro Bowl honors the next. But he soon moved inside and was a Pro Bowl performer at defensive tackle for the first time in the 1964 season, and for every year after that through 1973.

Over the course of his 14 seasons, Lilly bridged the gap between the Cowboys' teams that rarely won in his early years and the teams that rarely lost in his later years. With Lilly anchoring the "Doomsday Defense," Dallas began a record run of 20 consecutive winning seasons in 1966. The club reached its first Super Bowl in the 1970 season, then won the Super Bowl for the first time in the 1971 season, routing the Miami Dolphins 24-3 in game VI.

6 POINTS

- Teamed with Larry Cole to sack Miami's Bob Griese for a 29-yard loss in Super Bowl VI
- Scored four career TDs: three on fumble returns and one on an interception return
- Only player in Cowboys' history to wear number 74
- Never missed a regular season game in his 14 seasons
- Named to NFL's All-Decade Team of both 1960s and 1970s
- First inductee into the Cowboys' Ring of Honor (1975)

MERLIN OLSEN No. 27

LOS ANGELES RAMS

POSITION: DEFENSIVE TACKLE
YEARS: 1962–1976
HEIGHT: 6-5 WEIGHT: 270
SCHOOL: UTAH STATE
HALL OF FAME: 1982

Long before Merlin Olsen charmed television audiences as the genial Father Murphy or as a spokesman for a floral delivery service, he terrorized opposing quarterbacks and ballcarriers as the linchpin of the Los Angeles Rams' "Fearsome Foursome" defensive line of the late 1960s and early 1970s.

Olsen was the third overall pick of the 1962 NFL Draft, and before the preseason was over, the former Utah State star earned a full-time starting spot at defensive tackle. He went on to earn a Pro Bowl berth that year . . . and the year after that . . . and the year after that . . . ending up with an all-time, all-position record of 14 consecutive Pro Bowl selections. He retired following the 1976 season, but only after playing in all 14 regular season games for the 14th year in a row. In fact, he missed only two of 210 regular season games in his NFL career.

For much of Olsen's 15 seasons, he lined up alongside Rams end Deacon Jones, another member of the Pro Football Hall of Fame. While Jones made headlines for rushing the quarterback, Olsen could always be counted on to fill the gaps behind him. Tackle Roosevelt Grier and end Lamar Lundy were the other primary members of the "Fearsome Foursome," but it was Olsen who was the anchor of that famous unit.

The Rams reached the postseason six times in Olsen's 15 seasons, and they won the NFC West each of his final four years.

---

6 POINTS

- First- or second-team All-Pro selection 10 times
- Phi Beta Kappa scholar at Utah State
- Won Outland Trophy as college football's best interior lineman in 1961
- Began acting career while still an NFL player
- Played Jonathan Garvey on TV's *Little House on the Prairie*
- Starred in his own TV series, *Father Murphy*, from 1981 to 1983

No. 28

EMMITT SMITH

DALLAS COWBOYS
ARIZONA CARDINALS

POSITION: RUNNING BACK
YEARS: 1990–2004
HEIGHT: 5-9 WEIGHT: 210
SCHOOL: FLORIDA
HALL OF FAME: 2010

CAREER STATS				
Yrs.	Att.	Yds.	Yds./Carry	Rush TDs
15	4,409	18,355	4.2	164

Emmitt Smith wasn't blessed with the speed of Eric Dickerson or Tony Dorsett. He didn't have the elusiveness of Barry Sanders or Gale Sayers. And he didn't have the size of Jim Brown or Franco Harris. But Smith ran for more yards than all of those Pro Football Hall of Famers—indeed, more yards than anyone else in NFL history—because of an indomitable will and an unquenchable desire to compete at the highest level.

Case in point: Smith's Dallas Cowboys entered the final game of the 1993 season needing a victory over the New York Giants to win the NFC East and earn a bye in the opening round of the playoffs. One problem: Early in the second quarter, Smith separated his shoulder when he was tackled by Giants safety Greg Jackson after a long gain.

Smith gingerly headed to the sideline. For almost anyone else, that would have been the end of his day. After all, a running back can't keep an injured shoulder from getting hit. But after missing two snaps, he was back in game—and not as a decoy, either. Instead, Smith played through the pain on carry after carry. By the end of the day, he set a club record with 42 touches, on 32 carries and 10 receptions. He ran for 168 yards and gained 229 of the Cowboys' 339 total yards. Dallas prevailed 16–13 in overtime—Smith accounted for 41 of the team's 52 yards on its game-winning field goal drive—and, eventually, went on to win its second consecutive Super Bowl. (Smith was the MVP of the Cowboys' 30–13 victory over Buffalo in game XXVIII.)

Smith's big day against the Giants also sealed his third consecutive NFL rushing title. Two years later, he won another crown by rushing for 1,773 yards while helping the Cowboys to their third Super Bowl victory in a four-season span. He rushed for at least 1,000 yards a league-record 11 seasons in a row beginning in 1991, and in 2001 surpassed Jim Brown as the NFL's all-time leading rusher.

Smith reached the top spot by seeming to glide along the line of scrimmage behind the Cowboys' massive offensive linemen, then to pick just the right time to cut back and burst through an opening. He also got stronger as a game went on, and short gains in the first and second quarters often turned into big plays in the third and fourth.

After two seasons with the Arizona Cardinals, including a 937-yard, nine-touchdown effort at age 35 in 2004, Smith retired. His final totals: an NFL-record 18,355 rushing yards, 21,579 yards from scrimmage (No. 2 on the all-time list), and 175 total touchdowns (also No. 2 on the all-time list).

Two years later, Smith won television's *Dancing with the Stars* competition. (He was teamed with professional dancer Cheryl Burke.) Clearly, his competitive fire did not wane after he stepped off the football field.

6 POINTS

- Seventeenth overall pick of 1990 NFL Draft
- Earned eight Pro Bowl selections, including his first six seasons in the league
- Named NFL MVP for 1993 despite missing first two games that year
- Scored 25 TDs in 1995, then a single-season record
- Threw for a 21-yard TD in 2004 on lone pass attempt of his 15-year career
- Signed one-day contract with Dallas in February 2005 to officially retire as a Cowboy

No. 29 JACK LAMBERT

PITTSBURGH STEELERS

POSITION: LINEBACKER
YEARS: 1974–1984
HEIGHT: 6-4 **WEIGHT:** 220
SCHOOL: KENT STATE
 **HALL OF FAME:** 1990

O The heart and soul of the Pittsburgh Steelers' dynasty that won four Super Bowl championships in the 1970s was the "Steel Curtain" defense. And the heart and soul of that defense was linebacker Jack Lambert.

Lambert was a second-round draft pick out of Kent State in 1974, and his gap-toothed snarl soon became a symbol of the gritty, hard-working Steelers team that won the first championship in more than four decades of the franchise's history. Lambert was a rookie starter on that squad, and was the man in the middle of the defense for each of the club's three other league-championship teams that decade.

Like most middle linebackers of his era, Lambert possessed an abundance of strength and toughness. Unlike almost anyone else, however, he combined hard hitting with a quickness and athleticism rarely seen before at his position. Such a combination helped him pounce on 17 opponents' fumbles and intercept 28 passes in his 11 seasons. He earned a Pro Bowl berth each year from 1975 to 1983, and he was a first-team all-pro six times, including five seasons in a row beginning in 1979.

Despite all those numbers, though, Lambert is perhaps best remembered for an incident early in his career. It came in Super Bowl X against the Dallas Cowboys in his second NFL season. After Pittsburgh's Roy Gerela missed a short field goal try as time ran out in the first half, Cowboys safety Cliff Harris mocked the diminutive kicker by patting him on the helmet. Lambert responded by flinging Harris to the ground like a rag doll. The inspired Steelers roared back in the second half to win the game, 21–17.

6 POINTS
- NFL Defensive Rookie of the Year in 1974
- NFL Defensive Player of the Year in 1976
- Sealed Pittsburgh's win over the Rams in Super Bowl XIV with a fourth-quarter interception
- Steelers' defensive captain for his final eight years
- His number (58) hasn't been officially retired, but no Steelers player has worn it since he did
- Named to NFL's 75th Anniversary All-Time Team

NIGHT TRAIN LANE No. 30

LOS ANGELES RAMS
CHICAGO CARDINALS
DETROIT LIONS

POSITION: DEFENSIVE BACK
YEARS: 1952–1965
HEIGHT: 6-2 **WEIGHT:** 212
SCHOOL: SCOTTSBLUFF J.C.
HALL OF FAME: 1990

The story of how Dick Lane became a Hall of Fame defensive back reads like something made up in Hollywood. Actually, it started a little south of there, at the Rams' office in Los Angeles. Lane noticed the office during a bus ride to his job at an aircraft factory, and came back with a scrapbook that showed off his football experience. Though it's hard to believe in this day of intense scrutiny of every player from pee-wee up, the man who would set one of the NFL's longest-standing records (14 interceptions in the 12-game 1952 season) got his job by knocking on the door.

Lane had played in junior college and the Army, but didn't move to the pros, instead heading off to work like most former college players. The Rams found a home for him at defensive back, however, and he took the league by storm. He combined a nose for the ball (his 68 career picks are still fourth all-time) with ferocious tackling ability. He could fly, too. While doubling as a receiver with the Cardinals in 1955, he caught a team-record 98-yard TD.

Of course, Lane is also known for having one of the most famous nicknames in NFL history. He became the rhythmic and rhyming Night Train Lane after he was heard listening to a song by that name during his first Rams training camp. The Night Train's final stop, not surprisingly, was a spot in the Hall of Fame.

6 POINTS

- Previous experience included Scottsbluff J.C.
- Served four years in Army
- Scored five TDs on interception returns
- Also led NFL in 1954 with 10 interceptions
- Selected to seven Pro Bowls
- Led NFL in interception return yards in 1952 and 1954

BRUCE SMITH

BUFFALO BILLS

POSITION: DEFENSIVE END
YEARS: 1985–2003
HEIGHT: 6-4 WEIGHT: 280
SCHOOL: VIRGINIA TECH
HALL OF FAME: 2009

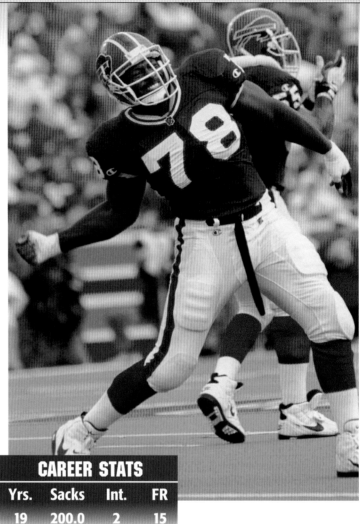

T o whom much is given, says the Good Book, much is expected. Bruce Smith was blessed with tremendous speed and quickness, developed strength and determination, and enjoyed an attitude that made him both infuriating to opponents and beloved by teammates.

Smith paid all of those gifts back . . . and then some.

The NFL's all-time leader in sacks helped the Bills win four AFC championships and earned 11 Pro Bowl selections. Such success was somewhat expected, since at Virginia Tech, he won the Outland Trophy and was a two-time All-America. Then the Bills made him the overall No. 1 draft pick in the 1985 draft, and installed him at right defensive end, where he began his assault on NFL QBs. Smith racked up 6.5 sacks and recovered four fumbles as a rookie in 1985, and—except for an injury-shortened season in 1991—he never had fewer than 10 sacks in a season until 1999. In all, he would have at least 10 sacks in 13 seasons, another NFL record.

As the Bills began their uphill climb from perennial cellar-dwellers to AFC elite, Smith's ability to draw multiple blockers on every play created mismatches that the Bills defense could exploit. Not that he didn't still get his sacks and tackles: through the Bills' championship years in the early 1990s, he had five seasons with 75 or more tackles.

In Smith's finest season, 1990, he had 19 sacks (ninth most in a season) and led the team to Super Bowl XXV. Smith gave them some much-needed points by sacking the Giants' Jeff Hostetler for a safety. However, the Bills lost after a long, final-play field goal was unsuccessful. The Bills made it to the next three Super Bowls, but lost all three, though Smith did his best to break that streak.

When you're essentially unblockable, you can boast about it. Smith's brash personality grated on opponents, but as they say, it's not bragging if you back it up. Though opposing offensive coaches knew

CAREER STATS			
Yrs.	Sacks	Int.	FR
19	200.0	2	15

they had to game-plan around Smith, he continued to dominate at the line, racking up double-digit sack totals and disrupting running games. (He recovered 15 fumbles in his career.) Smith also remained at a high level of skill and success for much longer than other defensive standouts. He was the NFL defensive player of the year in both 1990 and six seasons later in 1996.

He continued chasing Reggie White for the all-time sacks lead. Finally, in what would be his last season (2003), he got his 199th to set a new record, then added one more to set what is probably an unapproachable mark of 200. Only one active player, Jason Taylor, is within 70 sacks of Smith's mark through 2010.

6 POINTS

- Had 46 sacks in just three seasons at Virginia Tech
- 14.5 postseason sacks second-most all-time
- Scored just one TD, on a fumble recovery
- Named AFC defensive player of the year two times
- Named to NFL's All Decade Team of both 1980s and 1990s
- Ranked in the top ten in sacks eight times

"I consider it an insult if you don't block me with two players."

— Bruce Smith

TOP 10 DRAFT STEALS

1 TOM BRADY
Every team in the NFL passed on Brady . . . at least four times. With pick No. 199, the Patriots got three Super Bowls.

2 JOE MONTANA
Walsh knew Montana was his guy. He gambled and won the Super Bowl lottery in the third round.

3 TERRELL DAVIS
The Broncos struck gold in the sixth round in 1995, finding this eventual Super Bowl MVP and 2,000-yard runner.

4 DEACON JONES
The NFL Draft is only seven rounds now, not the 14 the Rams needed to find this Hall of Famer in 1961.

5 DAN MARINO

Elway and Jim Kelly went before Marino. Okay. But Todd Blackledge, Tony Eason, and Ken O'Brien? Marino was No. 6.

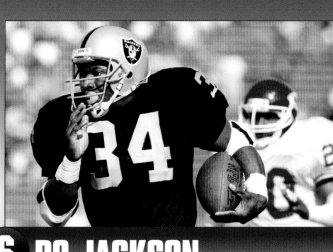

6 BO JACKSON

With an asterisk, since many folks *expected* Bo to know baseball. Didn't mean he didn't know football, too!

7 SHANNON SHARPE

One of the most successful tight ends of all time, and a 2011 Hall of Famer, Sharpe lasted until late in the seventh round.

8 RAY GUY

This isn't so much a steal as a reach. A punter in the first round? It made sense if he was to become the best ever.

9 LARRY WILSON

One of the toughest guys in NFL history had to tough it out until the seventh round in 1960.

10 ROGER STAUBACH

A post-college Navy stint scared off some teams, but the Cowboys knew that Roger the Dodger was worth the wait.

No. 32 JIM PARKER

BALTIMORE COLTS

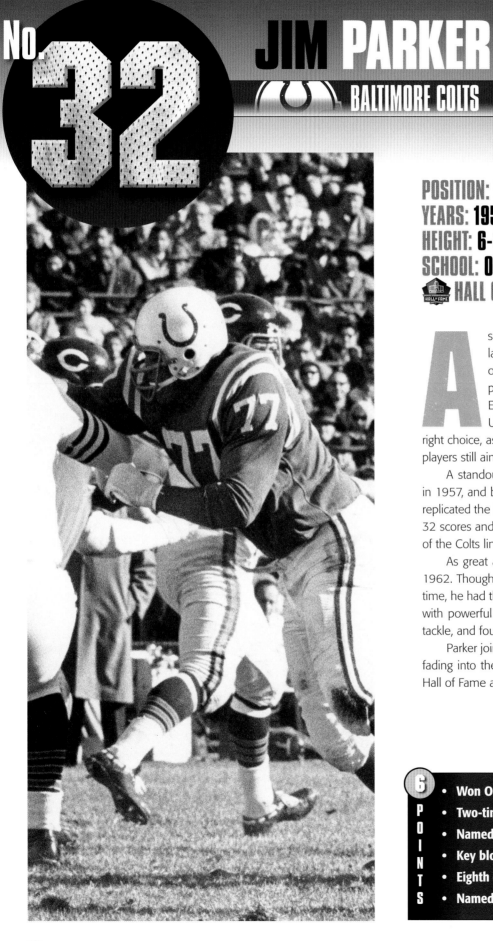

POSITION: GUARD/TACKLE
YEARS: 1957–1967
HEIGHT: 6-3 **WEIGHT:** 273
SCHOOL: OHIO STATE
 **HALL OF FAME:** 1973

As Johnny Unitas went, so went the Baltimore Colts of the late 1950s and early 1960s. The whole team—and all of its fans and coaches—knew that keeping the talented passer and leader healthy was vital. So head coach Weeb Ewbank gave the important job of left tackle, protecting Unitas's blind side, to big Jim Parker. Ewbank made the right choice, as Parker set standards for offensive line play that today's players still aim for.

A standout at Ohio State, Parker moved into the starting lineup in 1957, and by the following year, the Colts were NFL champs. They replicated the feat in 1959, as Parker's blocking helped Unitas pass for 32 scores and Alan Ameche run for seven more. He was the bedrock of the Colts line for all of his 11 seasons.

As great as he was at tackle, Parker was moved to left guard in 1962. Though he was one of the biggest players in the league at the time, he had the quickness to pull on sweeps and the strength to deal with powerful defensive tackles. He was All-NFL eight times—four at tackle, and four at guard.

Parker joined the NFL just as the days of the two-way player were fading into the past. He thus became the first person elected to the Hall of Fame after playing exclusively on the offensive line.

6 POINTS

- Won Outland Trophy at Ohio State
- Two-time All-America at tackle
- Named to eight consecutive Pro Bowls
- Key blocker during Unitas's 47-game TD-pass streak
- Eighth overall pick of 1957 NFL Draft
- Named guard on NFL's 75th Anniversary All-Time Team

SID LUCKMAN No.

CHICAGO BEARS

33

POSITION: QUARTERBACK
YEARS: 1939–1950
HEIGHT: 6-0 WEIGHT: 197
SCHOOL: COLUMBIA
HALL OF FAME: 1965

The NFL was undergoing a massive strategic change in the 1940s, and Sid Luckman was right at the center of it. The T-formation was coming into play after years of single-wing and other run-oriented offenses. In fact, Luckman had been a running QB in Columbia's single-wing. But he was thrust into the T by Bears coach George Halas when he joined Chicago in 1939.

Showing the versatility that would make him a Hall of Famer (and the brains that he needed to make it into the Ivy League), Luckman mastered the T. He and the Bears put it in the NFL playbook to stay with their famous 73–0 shellacking of the Redskins in the 1940 NFL Championship (a score that marks the most points ever scored in an NFL game). The Bears repeated in 1941, 1943, and 1946, with Luckman at the heart of all their titles.

In 1943, he set league records for touchdown passes (28) and passing yards (2,194). That season, he also became the first player with seven TD passes in one game, a record since matched but never beaten. (And it came on a day when the home-team Giants had honored him with Sid Luckman Day!) The 1946 championship was a thank-you present to the Bears. Luckman had been offered a huge sum to play for and coach the Chicago Rockets of the new AAFC. He turned it down, and instead won the NFL again. No doubt about it: his abilities helped turn the game of football from a ground game to an air attack, a change that continues to be seen today.

6 POINTS

- Worked as a lifeguard during collegiate summers
- Played defensive back and had 17 career interceptions
- Was also Bears' punter
- Threw five TD passes in 1943 NFL Championship Game
- Led NFL in TD passes and passing yards in 1943, 1945, and 1946
- Named first-team All-Pro five times

No. 34 DEION SANDERS

ATLANTA FALCONS
SAN FRANCISCO 49ERS
DALLAS COWBOYS
WASHINGTON REDSKINS
BALTIMORE RAVENS

POSITION: CORNERBACK
YEARS: 1989–2005
HEIGHT: 6-1 WEIGHT: 198
SCHOOL: FLORIDA STATE
HALL OF FAME: 2011

CAREER STATS			
Yrs.	Sacks	Int.	FR
14	1.0	53	13

What can you say about "Neon" Deion "Prime Time" Sanders that he probably hasn't said already himself? Sanders was one of the few athletes who not only made sure everyone was watching him . . . but he just about always came through when the spotlight shone brightest in his direction. Blessed with speed and amazingly quick moves, Sanders became one of the best (and some say the best) cover corners in NFL history. Teams simply planned to only throw on the half of the field away from Sanders. John Madden called him the "first player to be able to dominate a game from the defensive back position."

Not only was he such a great cornerback, he was also one of the most exciting kick returners in the game. With the Falcons early in his career, he carried back punts and kickoffs. He scored on returns in each of his first two seasons, and led the NFL with 1,067 kickoff-return yards in 1992, his fourth season. Even as late as 1998, at the age of 31, Sanders led the NFL in punt-return average, while scoring two more punt-return TDs.

Overall, Sanders scored touchdowns just about every way you can except rushing: punt return (a total of six), kickoff returns (three), interception return (nine), and fumble returns (one). During short stints as a receiver with Atlanta and Dallas, he also caught three touchdown passes.

Such versatility was nothing new for this amazing athlete. While he was with the Falcons, he was also an outfielder with the Atlanta Braves. He is the only person to play in a Super Bowl (XXX with Dallas)

and the World Series (1995 with Atlanta), and Sanders's teams won both, making him also the one person with championship rings from each sport. He was also part of the San Francisco 49ers Super Bowl XXIX championship. In 1989, he scored a touchdown for the Falcons and later hit a homer for the Braves in the same week, another first and only. His dual roles as receiver and defensive back in 1996 for Dallas made him the first player to go two ways regularly on the field since the early 1960s.

With such skills and accomplishments, Sanders found himself often the center of attention, and he was never shy about exploiting it. His public persona of the jewelry-flashing, touchdown-dancing, publicity-hungry athlete, however, was at odds with his private reputation among players as a clean-living, hard-working player. He was an easy pick for football writers as one of the newest members of the Hall of Fame, Class of 2011.

6 POINTS

- Won Jim Thorpe Trophy as top college defensive back
- Also helped Florida State reach College World Series
- Had career-high seven interceptions in 1993
- Led NFL with 303 interception return yards in 1994
- Named to Pro Bowl eight times
- Retired in 2001 but returned for 2004 and 2005 seasons with Baltimore

No. 35

CHUCK BEDNARIK

PHILADELPHIA EAGLES

POSITION: LINEBACKER/CENTER
YEARS: 1949–1962
HEIGHT: 6-3 **WEIGHT:** 233
SCHOOL: PENNSYLVANIA
 **HALL OF FAME:** 1967

How many storylines can one player have? Chuck Bednarik has a basketful. A standout linebacker for the Eagles, he also played center for many years, most famously playing 58 minutes of the 1960 NFL Championship Game, making all the snaps and stopping the Packers' Jim Taylor on the final play to seal the win.

Which leads to another storyline: His Eagles were the last Philly team to win the NFL title.

Bednarik's backstory provides another great tale. He moved from high school right into the U.S. Army during World War II. He flew 30 missions as a gunner on bombers soaring over Europe.

Which made him a pretty old freshman by the time he started at Penn after the war, but he showed what a veteran could do, earning a pair of All-America team berths at center. With Philadelphia, he was All-Pro as a center by his second season. From the mid-1950s onward, he played almost exclusively linebacker, earning eight Pro Bowl honors in his career. (His 1960 double-duty triumph came about due to injuries.)

Finally, NFL history fans remember him for the smashing hit he laid on Frank Gifford of the Giants—a hit so solid that Gifford missed the entire 1961 season.

The last of the 60-minute men, Bednarik was a bridge between generations, connected to the "Greatest Generation" through his war service, but still a force into the 1960s as the game moved permanently into specialization. However you tell it, Bednarik's is a unique and memorable tale.

6 POINTS

- First overall pick of 1949 NFL Draft
- Nicknamed "Concrete Charlie"
- Named MVP of 1954 Pro Bowl
- Made 20 interceptions, scored 1 TD
- Recovered 21 opponents' fumbles
- Named all-time center on NFL's 50th Anniversary All-Time Team in 1969

RAYMOND BERRY No. 36

BALTIMORE COLTS

POSITION: WIDE RECEIVER
YEARS: 1955–1977
HEIGHT: 6-2 **WEIGHT:** 185
SCHOOL: SOUTHERN METHODIST
HALL OF FAME: 1973

Name some things you need to be a great NFL receiver, and Raymond Berry didn't have a lot of them. He wasn't that fast. One of his legs was shorter than the other. He had terrible vision. He was about 20 pounds too light on a 6-2 frame.

But what Berry did have was an intense drive to succeed, an unmatched work ethic, and hands—some of the surest ever seen in the game.

Berry teamed on the Colts with Johnny Unitas to form one of the NFL's greatest passer-receiver combos. The two worked to foster an almost unconscious connection, a link that created some of the biggest plays in team history. It was Unitas-to-Berry to set up the winning touchdown in overtime in the 1958 NFL Championship Game, the "Greatest Game Ever Played." They matched the feat in 1959, though they didn't need overtime.

Berry practiced constantly, inventing new ways to learn his routes and his position. Berry talked Unitas into actually throwing *bad* passes to him after practice so that he could experience every possible outcome. Berry claimed to have 88 separate moves to use on defensive backs. He kept detailed notes on opponents and pass routes.

Though people who had written him off years earlier might not have believed it, Berry was the NFL's all-time leader with 631 catches when he retired in 1967. He went on to become a successful NFL coach, bringing the same intensity of study to the sidelines that he showed in practice and on the NFL playing field. In 1985, he led the Patriots to their first Super Bowl.

6 POINTS

- Named to six Pro Bowls
- Led NFL in receptions in 1958, 1959, and 1960
- Led NFL in TD catches in 1958 and 1959
- Colts' 20th-round future choice in 1954
- Led NFL in receiving yards in 1957, 1959, and 1960
- Had 51–41 record as coach of Patriots

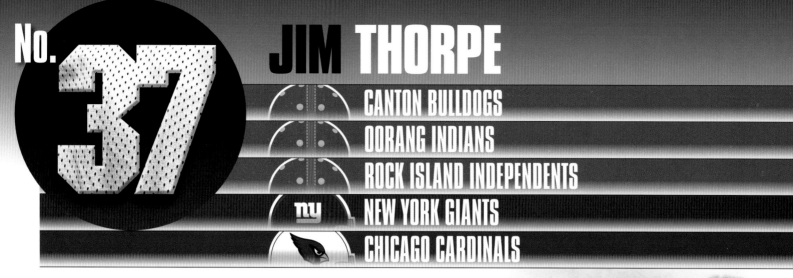

No. 37 JIM THORPE

CANTON BULLDOGS
OORANG INDIANS
ROCK ISLAND INDEPENDENTS
NEW YORK GIANTS
CHICAGO CARDINALS

POSITION: HALFBACK/DEFENSIVE BACK/KICKER
YEARS: 1920–1928
HEIGHT: 6-1 WEIGHT: 202
SCHOOL: CARLISLE INDIAN SCHOOL
HALL OF FAME: 1963

Entire books have been written about Jim Thorpe's amazing Olympic accomplishments—gold medals in the pentathlon and decathlon in 1912—and his record-setting college career (he scored all the points in a game in Carlisle's huge upset of Army and was a two-time All-America). His all-around athletic skills (*take that, Neon Deion!*) were so profound that he was named the Athlete of the Half-Century in 1950, and he remained near the top of the list at the end of the whole century!

However, he's honored today for his role in pro football, so let's concentrate here on Thorpe's NFL years.

When the league started in 1920, Thorpe was already a pro football veteran, having played for the Canton Bulldogs since 1915. In fact, some experts say that Thorpe's celebrity and gridiron prowess put pro football on the map and made the NFL possible. When he joined the semipro Bulldogs, he quadrupled attendance and allowed team owners to raise ticket prices by 30 percent. He was such a huge name that the NFL (known as the American Pro Football Association for its first two seasons) not only wanted him as a player, but also named him its first president. The job was ceremonial; his play was anything but.

Though he was 32 when the NFL started, Thorpe still had enough skill to be one of the top runners in the league. In those two-way days, he also played defensive back with ferocity. And he was one of the best ever at the drop-kick style then in use. His pregame exhibitions were legendary, as he would drop kick a field goal 50 yards in one direction . . . then turn around and aim at the other goalpost. Though he was past his prime, he was remembered by one opponent from those years as like "trying to tackle an oak tree."

CAREER STATS

Yrs.	Att.	Yds.	Yds./Carry	Rush TDs
8	n/a	n/a	n/a	6

In 1922, Thorpe left the Bulldogs to join an independent team of Native Americans, the Oorang Indians. The team was actually created as an advertising vehicle for an entrepreneur named Walter Lingo, but the upshot was employment for Native American athletes, led by

6 POINTS

- Won pentathlon and decathlon at 1912 Olympics
- 1911 and 1912 All-America at Carlisle
- Led Canton to unofficial titles in 1916, 1917, and 1919
- During exhibitions, kicked 50-yard drop-kick field goals
- Native American name Wa-Tho-Huk means "Bright Path"
- Named Greatest Athlete of the Half-Century in 1950

Thorpe, a member of the Sac and Fox Nation. Decades later, thanks to his many athletic exploits, Thorpe remains one of the most famous Native Americans ever. After the Indians folded in 1923, he played parts of three more seasons with other teams, finishing with a token appearance at the age of 40 in 1928.

Though he was never the on-field terror in the NFL that he was in college, Thorpe's skills placed him among the best players of the NFL's first decade, and his influence in making pro football acceptable was vital to the league's success.

No. 38 LANCE ALWORTH

SAN DIEGO CHARGERS
DALLAS COWBOYS

POSITION: WIDE RECEIVER
YEARS: 1962–1972
HEIGHT: 6-0 **WEIGHT:** 184
SCHOOL: ARKANSAS
HALL OF FAME: 1978

The American Football League emerged in 1960, started by some frustrated businessmen who were kept out of the NFL's exclusive club. The league soon gained a reputation for high-scoring, high-octane offenses. One of the biggest reasons was a guy they called Bambi.

"He made it look like a wide-open game," said AFL co-founder Lamar Hunt, "because he was always open."

Lance Alworth came to the AFL and the Chargers in 1962 as one of the early beneficiaries of a bidding war between the two leagues. San Diego coaxed the Arkansas star to head to Southern California instead of to the San Francisco 49ers of the NFL. After a year of settling in at receiver—as a halfback with Arkansas he had rarely caught passes—Alworth burst out in his second season and never stopped. That 1963 season was the first of seven straight 1,000-yard seasons and the first of five seasons reaching double digits in touchdown catches. His downfield skills played a big part in the Chargers' AFL title that year, which ended with a 51–10 pasting of Boston.

The numbers don't tell the whole story, though, since Alworth was revered for his speed, his leaping ability (hence the nickname, which he didn't actually like), and his post-catch running. Alworth was the whole package of speed and moves. After an amazing nine years with San Diego, he was traded to the Cowboys in 1971. He capped off his career by helping Dallas win Super Bowl VI. In fact, it was a TD catch by Alworth that helped propel the Cowboys to a 24–7 victory.

In 1978, Alworth was the first player from the AFL named to the Pro Football Hall of Fame. Many of this his fellow "football rebels" would follow him in the ensuing years, but none would make a bigger impact on that upstart league.

6 POINTS

- All-America halfback at Arkansas
- Named to seven AFL All-Star Games
- Caught at least one pass in 96 straight games
- Averaged more than 50 catches and 1,000 yards in San Diego career
- Led AFL in receptions in 1966, 1968, and 1969
- 18.9 yards per catch best all-time among receivers with 500 catches

GINO MARCHETTI No. 39

DALLAS TEXANS
BALTIMORE COLTS

POSITION: DEFENSIVE END
YEARS: 1952–1966
HEIGHT: 6-4 **WEIGHT:** 244
SCHOOL: SAN FRANCISCO
HALL OF FAME: 1972

Gino Marchetti was a fighter. Point him toward the fellow on the other side and get out of the way—that was all the instruction he needed. His first opponents were the more serious ones: German troops. Marchetti served with great distinction in the Army in Europe in WWII, facing heavy action. He put off college until the war was over, so by the time he made it to the pros, he was 25 years old.

Next up to face Gino: blockers and ballcarriers and quarterbacks. For someone who had survived the war, this was child's play. For the next 14 seasons, he won just about every battle he fought on the football field, tossing aside blockers "like rag dolls," as a respectful opponent once said. Marchetti was a terror on passing downs, causing havoc when he didn't have to worry about waiting for a runner to reach him.

He proved his toughness in one of the most famous games ever, the 1958 NFL Championship Game. Late in the game against the Giants, Marchetti made a key stop of Frank Gifford, but ended up with a leg broken in two places. Though doctors wanted him to head to the hospital, Marchetti insisted he stay on the sidelines—on the stretcher—until the game was over. He didn't want to leave his teammates. He bounced back from the injury to help the Colts win again in 1959.

Marchetti's 11 Pro Bowl selections are among the most ever for a defender. In 1969, he was named the top defensive end of the NFL's first 50 seasons. No one dared to fight him for the honor, of course.

6 POINTS

- Two-time All-America at San Francisco
- Named to 11 consecutive Pro Bowls
- Drafted by Dallas Texans in second round in 1952
- After Texans disbanded in 1952, wound up on expansion Colts' roster in 1953
- Played college football at USF with fellow Pro Football Hall of Famers Ollie Matson and Bob St. Clair
- Named to NFL's 50th and 75th Anniversary All-Time Teams

TOP 10 BALLHAWKS

1 EMLEN TUNNELL

Tunnell had at least seven interceptions in all but one of his first seven years; the one off year? He had six!

2 PAUL KRAUSE

He doesn't get the run of some of the guys on this page, but he did make more picks (81) than any other player.

3 ROD WOODSON

Woodson's greatest asset in racking up interceptions was his ability to use sprinter speed to break to the ball.

4 NIGHT TRAIN LANE

Lane's 14 interceptions (in a 12-game 1952 season) remains the standard in that department . . . more than 50 years later.

5 DEION SANDERS

"Neon Deion" drew footballs to his hands like the reporters who tracked him down for yet another great quote.

6 DICK LEBEAU

LeBeau terrorized opposing receivers with the Lions and then became one of the best defensive coaches ever.

7 RONNIE LOTT

Lott proudly carried a reputation for his hard hitting, but it was his game-breaking nose for the ball that created points.

8 DARREN SHARPER

Sharper was never happy with just an interception; he wanted to make every one a pick six. With 11, he did pretty well.

9 KEN RILEY

With nine seasons with five or more picks, Riley finished strong, nabbing eight in his final season, 1983.

10 ED REED

Reed turns picks into points, with the two longest interception return TDs of all time.

No. 40 O.J. SIMPSON

BUFFALO BILLS
SAN FRANCISCO 49ERS

POSITION: RUNNING BACK
YEARS: 1969–1977
HEIGHT: 6-1 **WEIGHT:** 212
SCHOOL: SOUTHERN CALIFORNIA
 **HALL OF FAME:** 1985

He lived the best of times, he lived the worst of times. An objective person can't divide the two parts of O.J. Simpson's life. Of his actions and choices after he left the football field, there's not much more to be said here. In no way belittling the tragedies and crimes, we'll look only at his exploits as one of the greatest running backs in league history.

Simpson was a stunning talent, there's no doubt about that. At USC, he won the 1968 Heisman Trophy. Though the Bills chose him with the first overall pick of the 1969 draft, they didn't hand him the ball and stand back. In fact, he was not the team's starting back until his fourth season.

Buffalo struggled throughout Simpson's career there. They posted only three winning records and earned one playoff bid from 1969–1977. But even though his team struggled, Simpson soared. His speed, elusiveness, and power were the perfect combination for a runner. He could make people miss, he could evade them, or he could run over them as the situation demanded. In his first full season as the starter, he led the NFL with 1,251 yards, the first of four NFL rushing titles he would earn.

In 1973, he did something no back had done in NFL history. His final carry of the season, against the Jets, gave him 2,003 yards, making him the first player to top that 2,000-yard mark. He led the league again in 1975 and 1976, becoming what some experts called the best running back of the decade.

After finishing his career with two seasons in San Francisco, Simpson moved into a life of acting, broadcasting, celebrity . . . and tragedy.

6 POINTS

- Two-time All-America at USC
- Named to six Pro Bowls
- Also returned kickoffs in first four seasons
- Player of the game in 1973 Pro Bowl
- Led NFL in rushing in 1972, 1973, 1975, and 1976
- Acted in movies and worked on Monday Night Football

ROD WOODSON No. 41

PITTSBURGH STEELERS
OAKLAND RAIDERS

POSITION: CORNERBACK/SAFETY
YEARS: 1987–2003
HEIGHT: 6-0 WEIGHT: 200
SCHOOL: PURDUE
HALL OF FAME: 2009

f Rod Woodson had just stuck to cornerback, he'd have been a shoo-in Hall of Fame selection. Had he chosen to make his career solely returning punts and kickoffs, he might have gone to Canton just for that. That he was Hall-of-Fame caliber at two (some might say three) different disciplines says volumes about his all-around athleticism and football talent.

As a defensive back, Woodson was outstanding in coverage and a serious full-time ballhawk. His 71 interceptions are third most all-time, while his 12 touchdowns and 1,483 return yards both remain the all-time best. He had one interception in his first season, 1987 with Pittsburgh, and then never had less than three in a year until his final campaign, 2003 with Oakland (sans 1995, when he played just one game due to injury). His closing speed gave him a weapon against even the fleetest wide receivers, while his football instincts to be where the play was were unmatched. Woodson was selected to 11 Pro Bowls.

As a kick returner, he was electric. He made almost a science of the effort, mixing speed with moves and daring. Although he stopped returning kicks when he turned 30, leaving those to younger men, he set very high standards. He led the NFL in kickoff-return average in 1989, while scoring four career touchdowns on punt and kickoff returns.

A world-class hurdler at Purdue, his speed was his greatest weapon. However, a 1995 knee injury slowed him dramatically. On guts and guile, he played eight more seasons, showing he had more than enough weapons in his quiver.

6 POINTS

- Named to NFL's 75th Anniversary All-Time Team
- Named NFL Defensive Player of the Year in 1993
- Had career-long 98-yard "pick six" in 2002
- Made 32 fumble recoveries
- Had career high eight interceptions in 2002 at age 37
- Also had 13.5 sacks

No. 42

JOHN MACKEY

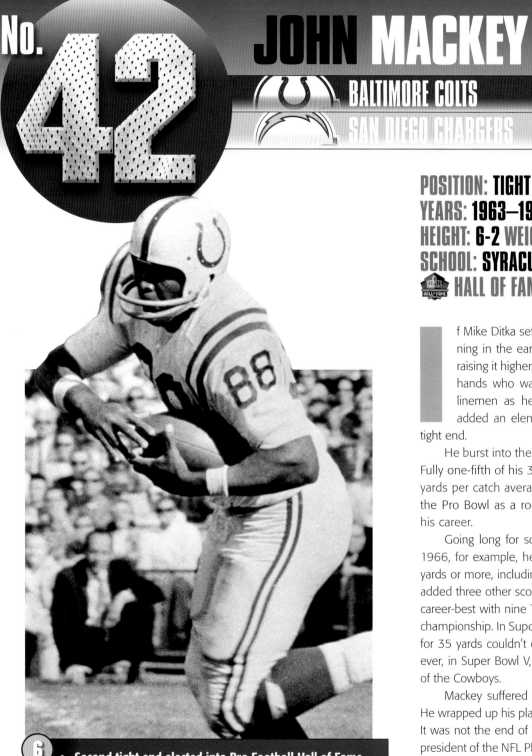

BALTIMORE COLTS
SAN DIEGO CHARGERS

POSITION: TIGHT END
YEARS: 1963–1972
HEIGHT: 6-2 WEIGHT: 224
SCHOOL: SYRACUSE
HALL OF FAME: 1992

f Mike Ditka set the bar for a new way to use tight ends beginning in the early 1960s, John Mackey took that bar and kept raising it higher. Like Ditka, he was a tall, rangy player with great hands who was equally at home pushing around defensive linemen as he was swooping downfield. Mackey, however, added an element of speed that had never been seen in a tight end.

He burst into the NFL in 1963 after a terrific career at Syracuse. Fully one-fifth of his 35 catches went for touchdowns, and his 20.7 yards per catch average proved to be a career high. He also made the Pro Bowl as a rookie, the first of five he would play in during his career.

Going long for scores proved to be a hallmark of his game. In 1966, for example, he scored six touchdowns that each traveled 50 yards or more, including a season- and career-high 89-yard score. He added three other scores that year of a more standard variety to set a career-best with nine TDs. In 1968, he helped the Colts win the NFL championship. In Super Bowl III that year, even Mackey's three catches for 35 yards couldn't overcome the destiny of the Jets' victory. However, in Super Bowl V, his long TD catch was key to the Colts' defeat of the Cowboys.

Mackey suffered knee injuries that dimmed his glorious speed. He wrapped up his playing career in 1972 with a season in San Diego. It was not the end of his football life, however. He had been elected president of the NFL Players' Association in 1970 and continued in that role through 1973. In fact, it was his lawsuit against some of the restrictive free-agency rules—*Mackey vs. NFL*—that brought about some of the key contract changes between owners and players in the 1970s.

6 POINTS

- Second tight end elected into Pro Football Hall of Fame
- Returned nine kickoffs during rookie season
- Had career-high 829 receiving yards in 1966
- Had career-high nine TDs in 1966
- 75-yard TD catch in Super Bowl V was longest until Super Bowl XV
- Top college tight end is given the annual John Mackey Award

ALAN PAGE No.

MINNESOTA VIKINGS
CHICAGO BEARS

43

POSITION: DEFENSIVE TACKLE
YEARS: 1967–1978
HEIGHT: 6-4 **WEIGHT:** 245
SCHOOL: NOTRE DAME
HALL OF FAME: 1988

Alan Page was born in Canton, Ohio, so it was only fitting that he ended up there after his NFL career was over. This outstanding defensive player made it to the Hall of Fame (located in Canton, of course) after a long and very productive career.

Page was an All-America defensive end at Notre Dame, but moved to the interior of the D-line in the pros. He became a starter with Minnesota early in his rookie season of 1967 and anchored a defense that soon became known as the "Purple People Eaters." The Vikings earned trips to five NFL/NFC title games and four Super Bowls. Though they lost all four of those Super Bowls, their run of dominance on D was impressive.

For his part, Page was one of the quickest defensive tackles ever. His speed to the point of attack was legendary, and his ability to out-maneuver offensive linemen challenged the typical wisdom that the key to reaching the quarterback was strength. Sacks were not official for most of his career, but some sources give him more than 170. He had an NFL-leading (and career-high) seven fumble recoveries in 1970, part of his career total of 23 such plays.

Page was so effective that he was named the 1971 NFL MVP, one of only two defensive players given that honor. He was also named the 1971 NFL defensive player of the year. Along the way, he earned nine straight Pro Bowl selections.

In 1978, after 12 seasons with the Vikings, he was waived and then joined the archrival Bears. Upon retiring in 1981, he embarked on one of the most distinguished post-NFL careers in recent decades. After earning his law degree, he became a judge and eventually earned a spot on the Minnesota Supreme Court.

6 POINTS
- Helped Notre Dame win 1966 national championship
- Two safeties in 1971 tied all-time best
- Tied for third with three career safeties
- Blocked 28 opponents' kicks
- Named All-NFL six times
- Elected to Minnesota Supreme Court

No. 44 MEL BLOUNT

PITTSBURGH STEELERS

POSITION: CORNERBACK
YEARS: 1970–1983
HEIGHT: 6-3 WEIGHT: 205
SCHOOL: SOUTHERN
HALL OF FAME: 1989

Y ou know you're a really effective and successful player if they change the rules to make your job even harder— as was the case with outstanding Steelers cornerback Mel Blount.

You wouldn't have guessed that would be in Blount's future after his first two miserable seasons in the NFL. He joined the Steelers in 1970 out of Southern University and found the adjustment to the NFL difficult. A particularly painful memory was watching fellow future Hall-of-Famer Paul Warfield score three times in a 1971 game, mostly while being "guarded" by Blount. Blount even considered quitting.

He stuck with it, however, changing mistakes into lessons. The following season, he didn't allow a single touchdown. He found that his strong, 6-3 frame was perfect for bump-and-run coverage and physical downfield play. By 1975, he was the NFL defensive player of the year and part of the famed Steel Curtain defense that helped the Steelers win four Super Bowls.

Blount was a big part of that championship run. His fumble recovery in the 1979 AFC Championship Game propelled the Steelers to the winning score. In Super Bowl XIII, a tightly contested game, the Steelers rallied to win after Blount made a key interception of a Cowboys pass. He also had a pick in Super Bowl IX, the first of his team's championships.

Blount's greatest skill on the field was using his speed (he ran a 4.5 40-yard dash when he was 35!) and strength to both stick with receivers downfield and jam them at the line. Trouble was, he was getting too good at it and inspiring others to try his techniques. In 1978, the NFL changed the rules about bump-and-run, limiting defensive backs to a single "bump" before releasing receivers to run downfield. (Later adjustments limited contact to five yards from scrimmage.) The

CAREER STATS			
Yrs.	Sacks	Int.	FR
14	n/a	57	13

"Blount Rule" made it easier on receivers to get separation and room to maneuver and harder on players like Blount, who now had to wait until the football arrived to initiate any more contact. He responded to the challenge as he had in 1971, and was named to three Pro Bowls after the rule was put in place. He retired in 1983 as the Steelers' all-time leader in interceptions with 57. More than 25 years later, he still stands atop that list.

- Missed only one game in 14-year career
- Was Steelers' kickoff returner occasionally
- Led NFL with 11 interceptions in 1975
- Had at least one interception in each of his 14 NFL seasons
- First-team All-Pro in 1975 and 1981
- Named to NFL's 75th Anniversary All-Time Team

Blount's all-around skills as a prototypical cornerback—and game-changing defender—later earned him a place on the NFL's 75th Anniversary All-Time Team, chosen in 1994. Since his retirement, he has become a champion cutting-horse rider, while also spending countless hours working at the Mel Blount Youth Home, a ranch in Georgia created to help boys facing difficult home or community lives.

45

TONY GONZALEZ

KANSAS CITY CHIEFS
ATLANTA FALCONS

POSITION: TIGHT END
YEARS: 1997–
HEIGHT: 6-5 WEIGHT: 251
SCHOOL: CALIFORNIA

I f you go by the numbers, it's an easy call: Tony Gonzalez is the best tight end in NFL history. If you go by intangibles—skill set, impact on games and team success, groundbreaking abilities—well, you can easily come to the same conclusion. No tight end has caught more passes for more yards and more touchdowns that the former Cal basketball star.

Gonzalez was a powerful inside rebounding force for the Golden Bears, while also blossoming into one of the nation's top receivers as a junior. The Chiefs made him the 13th overall pick of the 1997 draft, and by his second season he had reached the 50-catch plateau. He burst upward in 1999 with 11 touchdowns and the first of his 10 Pro Bowl selections (a record for tight ends, naturally). He topped 1,000 yards receiving for the first time in 2000, a mark he would reach three more times through 2010. From 1999 onward, he also never fell below 63 catches in a season through 2010.

Gonzalez's height combined with his basketball-based athleticism turned him into a go-to receiver, too fast for linebackers to cover and too big for defensive backs to shut down. His move to Atlanta in 2009 helped turn that team into a playoff contender, as he became a key outlet for young quarterback Matt Ryan. Every catch made from Ryan just adds to an historic record that will no doubt send Gonzalez to Canton when he's done.

6 POINTS

- All-America TE at Cal; helped basketball team reach Sweet 16 in 1997
- No other player has surpassed his 50 or more catches in 13 straight years
- Only tight end with eight 900-yard seasons
- First tight end with six 100-yard games in a season
- Led NFL in receptions (102) in 2004
- Career-high 11 TDs in 1999

ROGER STAUBACH No.

DALLAS COWBOYS

46

POSITION: QUARTERBACK
YEARS: 1969–1979
HEIGHT: 6-3 WEIGHT: 197
SCHOOL: NAVY
HALL OF FAME: 1985

Cowboys fans must wonder what might've happened had Roger Staubach not given the first four years of his post-college life to the United States Navy. Then again, it might have been the loyalty, leadership, and determination that he learned at the Naval Academy and in the service that helped mold him into a passer who led Dallas to its first two Super Bowl titles.

Staubach was a revelation as a midshipman at Navy, winning the 1963 Heisman Trophy with an all-out style that mixed in almost as much running as passing. Dallas drafted him knowing that he would fulfill his commitment to the service, so Staubach was 27 when he became an NFL rookie in 1969. By 1971, he was the starter and the NFL passing champion and had led Dallas to victory in Super Bowl VI. He was the MVP of the game with a pair of touchdown passes.

Worth the wait indeed.

"Roger the Dodger" used elusive scrambling and pinpoint passing to drive the Cowboys for eight more seasons, including their second NFL title in Super Bowl XII. He became almost as famous for his come-from-behind scrambles as for his backfield scampers. In 14 games, he led the Cowboys from behind in the final two minutes. In fact, in a 1975 playoff game, his last-minute heave to Drew Pearson was the first to be called a "Hail Mary" pass.

Since retiring, Staubach has become a successful real estate developer. He remains an idol to Cowboys fans and carried the Super Bowl trophy onto the field after Super Bowl XLV in Dallas in 2011.

6 POINTS

- Last military academy player to win Heisman Trophy
- Navy career included service in Vietnam
- Led NFL in TD passes (23) in 1973
- Led NFL in passer rating four times; high of 104.8 in 1971
- Retired with 83.4 passer rating, highest to that point
- Scored 20 rushing TDs

No. 47 RAY NITSCHKE

GREEN BAY PACKERS

POSITION: LINEBACKER
YEARS: 1958–1972
HEIGHT: 6-3 **WEIGHT:** 235
SCHOOL: ILLINOIS
HALL OF FAME: 1978

If you were trying to explain to an alien what an NFL player should look like, the classic exemplar of the species, you wouldn't go far wrong by showing him Ray Nitschke. The Packers' mighty middle linebacker exuded determination. Was it the missing teeth? The massive jawline set in a grimace of focused attention? The way he seemed to be muddy as soon as the game began? It was all that and more. In fact, Nitschke was so dominant and so feared that he was named the NFL's all-time top linebacker in 1969 . . . while he was still playing!

The former Illinois standout was the centerpiece of the powerful defense that Vince Lombardi, a former "block of granite" himself, built soon after arriving in Green Bay. Nitschke flew to the ball, showing surprising quickness for such a big man. He managed to snag 25 interceptions even though he wore massive pads and hand wraps. He was part of all five of the Packers' NFL championship teams, including both of the first two Super Bowls.

Off the field, however, his fierce appearance was muted by a quiet air and eyeglasses; quarterback Bart Starr once said that his teammate was like "Dr. Jekyll and Mr. Hyde." But once the good doctor put his teeth in a jar in his locker, slammed a helmet on his bald dome, and strapped on the pads and familiar No. 66, Mr. Hyde took over and caused havoc.

6 POINTS

- Also played fullback at Illinois
- Named MVP of 1962 NFL Championship Game
- Snared 25 interceptions, returned two for TDs
- Recovered 23 fumbles
- Named first-team All-Pro in 1964 and 1966
- First defensive player from Packers' title teams in Hall of Fame

RED GRANGE No. 48
CHICAGO BEARS

POSITION: RUNNING BACK/DEFENSIVE BACK
YEARS: 1925–1934
HEIGHT: 6-0 WEIGHT: 180
SCHOOL: ILLINOIS
HALL OF FAME: 1963

It's not much of a stretch to say that Red Grange saved the NFL. Already a national legend thanks to his exploits at Illinois, Grange's decision to play in the then-fledgling NFL catapulted the league and its teams into legitimacy.

At Illinois, Grange earned the immortal nickname "The Galloping Ghost." He was a three-time All-America and his long, twisting, tackle-breaking runs were newsreel staples. One of his most famous games was against Michigan: He scored long touchdowns the first four times he touched the ball. He also threw a TD pass.

Bears owner George Halas convinced Grange to join his team in an era when many college stars didn't bother with the rough-and-tumble NFL. Grange was an instant hit with fans, attracting more than 65,000 attendees to a game in New York a few years after his final game with the Illini. Almost overnight, the NFL became something to watch. Not only the Bears but the whole league gained fans and attention, thanks to Grange.

Grange and his agent, C.C. Pyle, took advantage of the Ghost's popularity by creating games for him to play in . . . and then raking home most of the gate. Their 17-game barnstorming tour led them to try starting their own pro league in 1926; Grange played for the New York Yankees of that league.

Though Grange's games did well, the new league soon flopped, and he returned to the Bears in 1927. A 1928 knee injury put an end to most of his most amazing feats, though he played until 1934. In his later seasons, he was also a terrific defensive back in those two-way days. For turning American sports fans' eyes firmly toward the NFL, Red Grange remains an iconic figure in the early history of the game.

6 POINTS

- Made his No. 77 jersey famous
- In Illinois upset of Penn, had 363 total yards
- Scored only TD as Bears beat Portsmouth in 1932 to win NFL
- Made key tackle to clinch 1933 NFL Championship Game
- Intercepted seven passes in 1934
- Member of inaugural class of Pro Football Hall of Fame

No. 49 MIKE HAYNES

NEW ENGLAND PATRIOTS
OAKLAND RAIDERS

POSITION: CORNERBACK
YEARS: 1976–1989
HEIGHT: 6-2 **WEIGHT:** 192
SCHOOL: ARIZONA STATE
 **HALL OF FAME:** 1997

Mike Haynes got off to a hot start in the NFL and didn't really cool off until he retired as one of the most respected defensive players of his era.

Haynes was the Patriots' number-one selection in 1976. After picking off eight passes and leading the AFC in punt-return yards, he was named the defensive rookie of the year. He also became the first player in Patriots history to score on a punt return . . . and he did it twice. He was named to the Pro Bowl, a rare honor for a rookie.

Over the next few seasons, Haynes used his great speed and study of the game to become one of the most feared defensive backs in the league. His number of interceptions went down for the simple reason that teams stopped throwing to his side of the field unless they really had to. He kept returning punts, though not as often, as his value as a defender increased.

Unlike some of his contemporaries, such as Mel Blount, Haynes was not a fierce or intimidating player; rather, he was more stylish, using closing speed more than hard hits.

After moving to Oakland in 1983, Haynes got one thing that had eluded him amid his accomplishments in New England: a Super Bowl ring. The Raiders won Super Bowl XVIII, helped by Haynes's interception of a pass by Joe Theismann of Washington. Earlier that season, he had also set an Oakland record with a 97-yard interception-return touchdown.

6 POINTS

- Three-year All-WAC star at Arizona State
- As rookie in 1976, returned two punts for TDs
- Also recovered 14 fumbles in career
- Led NFL in interception return yards (220) in 1984
- Selected to nine Pro Bowls, including each of first five seasons
- Named to NFL's 75th Anniversary All-Time Team in 1994

TERRY BRADSHAW No. 50

PITTSBURGH STEELERS

POSITION: QUARTERBACK
YEARS: 1970–1983
HEIGHT: 6-3 **WEIGHT:** 215
SCHOOL: LOUISIANA TECH
HALL OF FAME: 1989

6 POINTS

- Led NCAA in total yards as a junior
- Named NFL MVP for 1978
- Selected for three Pro Bowls
- Led NFL in TD passes in 1978 and 1982
- Also scored 32 rushing touchdowns
- Threw nine TD passes in Super Bowls

Most fans of recent vintage know Terry Bradshaw as the brash, blond, speak-the-truth analyst on CBS. But he earned his deserved place in the NFL 100 for having one of the most successful careers of the past few decades. Bradshaw was the driving force of the offense that carried the Steelers to four Super Bowl titles, the first team to reach that level.

He had a lot of pressure on his shoulders as the number-one overall draft pick out of Louisiana Tech in 1970. (The Steelers ended up with him after winning a coin flip with the Bears to determine which team got the first pick.) Though he was handed the reins by coach Chuck Noll very soon after joining the team, Bradshaw struggled in his first few seasons. By 1972, however, his power passing and his play calling, integrating the solid running of Franco Harris and the speed of receivers Lynn Swann and John Stallworth, led the Steelers to their first playoff win in team history. The team's 11–3 record that year was the first of an amazing streak for Bradshaw: He never again played for a pro team that had a losing season record in games he started.

By 1974, the Steelers were AFC champs. They won Super Bowl IX thanks in large part to the Steel Curtain defense. Bradshaw never topped 2,100 passing yards in that season nor in the team's Super Bowl X campaign. However, for the second part of their quartet of titles, Bradshaw's passing power moved to the forefront. He led the NFL in touchdowns in 1978 while setting a career high with 3,724 passing yards in 1979. Pittsburgh won Super Bowls after both of those seasons, and Bradshaw earned back-to-back Super Bowl MVP awards.

While his post-career success has given him a reputation for a bit of goofiness, his NFL career was one of outstanding success.

TOP 10 DUAL THREATS

1 SAMMY BAUGH
Two was not enough for Baugh: He was a league leader in passing, interceptions, and punting . . . in one year (1943).

2 BILL DUDLEY
Dudley led the NFL in rushing twice, had 23 interceptions, returned punts, kicks, and, in his spare time, punted.

3 FRANK GIFFORD
A star as a runner, receiver, and defensive back, Gifford was an intial-fest: HB, FL, WR, CB, S, and KR.

4 DEION SANDERS
Though Sanders was a rare NFL-MLB double-dipper, he's here for his mix of defensive stardom and returning skill.

5 ROD WOODSON

Woodson might have made the Hall of Fame as either a defensive back or a kick returner; he was that good at both.

6 GALE SAYERS

Sayers led the NFL in rushing yards twice, kickoff return yards three times, and tacklers flummoxed every season.

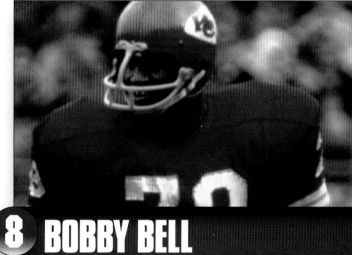

7 CHUCK BEDNARIK

Football's last (nearly) 60-minute man, Concrete Charlie was an all-pro at both linebacker and center.

8 BOBBY BELL

Bell makes this top 10 for being an all-state quarterback plus a defensive end in college before his NFL LB career.

9 GEORGE CONNOR

Connor could do it all without the ball: He was all-pro at both tackle and defensive tackle, as well as linebacker.

10 ERIC METCALF

Metcalf had double-digit career TD totals in rushing, receiving, and punt returns, plus a couple more on kickoffs.

No. 51 BART STARR
GREEN BAY PACKERS

POSITION: QUARTERBACK
YEARS: 1956–1971
HEIGHT: 6-1 **WEIGHT:** 197
SCHOOL: ALABAMA
HALL OF FAME: 1977

In the midst of generational change in the 1960s, Bart Starr was the model of "old school." He won five NFL championships as the Packers' quarterback, but while other players were starting to woof and raise their fingers, Starr just kept his calm, cool manner. While the press looked for the personalities of sports, Starr did his best work behind the scenes, working with the legendary Vince Lombardi to lead the Packers to victory after victory. While fans from afar might look askance at Starr's contributions (he never topped 16 TD passes or 2,500 passing yards in a season), his teammates to a man point to Starr as a huge reason for the Packers' unnervingly consistent success. A stat in point: His career postseason passer rating of 104.8 is 10 points higher than Joe Montana's.

Starr joined the Packers in 1956 after a solid career at Alabama. He played sparingly for most of his first four seasons. In 1960, Lombardi made him the full-time starter, and the confidence that gave Starr let him start building his offense in his own image. Remember, though Lombardi directed the team, this was back in the era when quarterbacks called the plays on the field.

The most famous play Starr called came in the 1967 NFL Championship Game, the famous "Ice Bowl." The Packers had already won two straight NFL titles but were trailing in the final minute against Dallas in arctic conditions. Facing a third-and-goal at the one, and with no timeouts left, Starr decided to take matters into his own hands. Behind a final surge from the Packers' line, he dove into the end zone with 13 seconds remaining for the winning score. Starr went on to lead the Packers to victories in the first two Super Bowls, putting a final cap on the great Green Bay decade.

CAREER STATS

Yrs.	W-L	Yds.	TD	Rating
16	94-57-6	24,718	152	80.5

- Was Packers' 17th-round draft pick in 1956
- Led NFL in completion percentage three times
- Had 9–1 record in postseason games
- Named NFL MVP for 1966
- Won MVP award in Super Bowl I and II
- Had streak of 294 passes without an interception

No. 52 ERIC DICKERSON

LOS ANGELES RAMS
INDIANAPOLIS COLTS
OAKLAND RAIDERS
ATLANTA FALCONS

POSITION: RUNNING BACK
YEARS: 1983–1993
HEIGHT: 6-3 WEIGHT: 220
SCHOOL: SOUTHERN METHODIST
HALL OF FAME: 1999

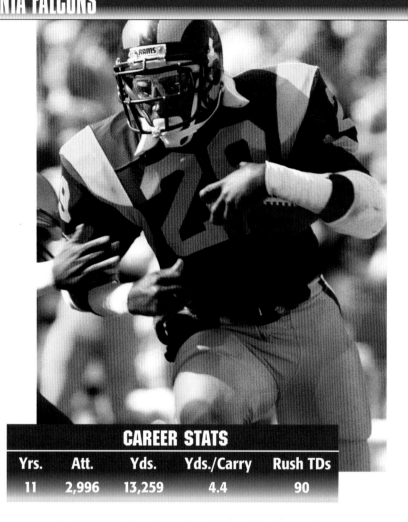

First, you're blinded by the numbers. Gaudy, simply gaudy. Eric Dickerson's 2,105 rushing yards in 1984 remain the standard other players are shooting for. Since he piled that total up for the Rams, four players have topped 2,000 yards, but none have topped Dickerson. In 11 seasons, he pounded out 13,259 yards, good for second all-time when he retired.

Next, you're distracted by the goggles, the neck brace, and the elbow pads. No one had ever worn goggles to play before Dickerson; they became a big part of his identity. However, after he retired, he described the goggles as ugly: "I hated wearing them, but I needed them to see." (In 2010, when Steven Jackson was set to break Dickerson's Rams' team rushing record, the younger player wore goggles in his honor.) The neck brace and pads were just protection—when you carry the ball more than 300 times in five different seasons (and 292 and 283 in two others), you're going to deal with some contact.

Numbers and unique eyewear sometimes obscure Dickerson's literally groundbreaking techniques and skill. At 6-3, he was much taller than most backs, but still had knee-buckling moves and breakaway speed. He presented a big target for defenders, but he hit holes with those high knees pumping and was very difficult to bring down.

He arrived in Los Angeles after a fantastic career at SMU, and yet exceeded expectations in a record-breaking way. His 1,808 rushing yards and 18 TDs on the ground were both the best ever for a first-year player. With such a start, you might expect a letdown . . . after all, he wasn't a surprise to opponents anymore. However, in 1984, he set the NFL single-season record that also still stands. He won two more NFL rushing titles in his career and never had less than 1,234 yards in any of his first seven seasons.

CAREER STATS

Yrs.	Att.	Yds.	Yds./Carry	Rush TDs
11	2,996	13,259	4.4	90

In 1987, already a three-time NFL rushing champ, he was sent to the Colts in one of the biggest midseason trades ever. He became a 1,000-yard runner for Indy even though he played only nine games for them. He helped them reach the playoffs for the first time in 10 years. The following years, he became the fastest ever to reach 10,000 career yards. Over his first seven years, he averaged better than 100 yards per game. You read that right . . . seven seasons.

By 1990, he was slowing down, and he spent single seasons with the Falcons and Raiders to close out his illustrious career. He remains among the very best ever to run with the football, and the best all alone for one season.

No. 53 WILLIE LANIER

KANSAS CITY CHIEFS

POSITION: LINEBACKER
YEARS: 1967–1977
HEIGHT: 6-1 WEIGHT: 245
SCHOOL: MORGAN STATE
HALL OF FAME: 1986

The 1950s and 1960s showcased some of the best middle linebackers in NFL history. Just flip through these pages and you'll find Butkus, Nitschke, Schmidt, Bednarik . . . those guys all shared with Willie Lanier toughness, football smarts, and a love of the solid tackle. What made Lanier unique was his heritage: He was the first African-American to hold down the key defensive position.

Lanier came to Kansas City in 1967 after starring at tiny Morgan State. Few gave him a chance to make an immediate impact. But coach Hank Stram said, "We don't care what color a player is . . . if he's good enough, he'll make our 40-man roster." Lanier did more than just make the team; he was the starting middle linebacker four games into his rookie season. He held the job for 11 years, earning six Pro Bowl selections as well as making a pair of All-AFL teams before the 1970 merger.

Lanier's biggest career highlight came in Super Bowl IV. After knocking off the defending AFL champion Jets, and then the Raiders, to make the big game, the Chiefs beat Minnesota 23–7. The Chiefs' defense, led by Lanier and fellow future Hall of Famer Bobby Bell, allowed the Vikings only 67 yards rushing. In one sequence in the fourth quarter, Lanier made two straight tackles . . . and then a key interception.

Nicknamed "Contact" for his love of a good tackle, Lanier combined speed and strategic intelligence to find himself time and again in the right spot to make that nickname come to life.

6 POINTS

- Member of NFL's 75th Anniversary All-Time Team
- Named NFL Man of the Year for 1972
- Missed only one game in final 10 seasons
- Made 27 career interceptions
- Recovered 18 fumbles
- Named defensive MVP of 1972 Pro Bowl

FORREST GREGG No.

GREEN BAY PACKERS
DALLAS COWBOYS

POSITION: TACKLE
YEARS: 1956–1971
HEIGHT: 6-4 **WEIGHT:** 249
SCHOOL: SOUTHERN METHODIST
HALL OF FAME: 1977

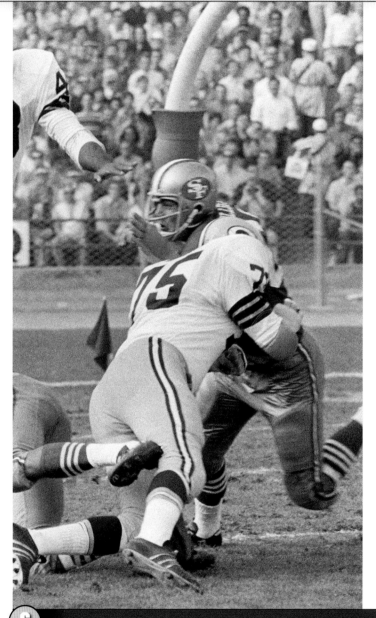

Vince Lombardi saw a lot of pretty impressive football talent over his many NFL days. But from all the star running backs to MVP quarterbacks to Hall of Fame defenders, he chose another figure as "the finest player I ever coached": Forrest Gregg anchored the Packers' offensive line throughout the team's amazing run in the 1960s. Without Gregg as part of the famed "Packers' Sweep" play, a key part of the Green Bay offense would not have worked. Tall, very strong, and durable (he played in 188 straight games in one long stretch), Gregg became the model of the offensive tackle that others aimed for.

He came to Green Bay in 1956 and began to study his opponents as he was back in class at SMU. He used film study to learn defenders' moves, and then he would practice counters to all of them. Coaches and opponents alike praised his exacting technique and picture-perfect form. He was also good enough to switch to guard in parts of two seasons, all without missing a beat. He was part of the Packers' five NFL title teams in the 1960s and was on the winning side in Super Bowls I and II.

Gregg brought greatness with him when he joined the Dallas Cowboys for his final season in 1971. He made it to his seventh championship game and earned his third Super Bowl ring as Dallas won Super Bowl V.

Gregg went on to a coaching career that included stops at Cleveland, Cincinnati, and Green Bay. He became the first former Super Bowl winner to coach a team in the Super Bowl, leading the 1981 Bengals to an AFC championship.

6 POINTS

- Played offensive and defensive tackle at SMU
- Missed 1957 season due to military service
- Named to nine Pro Bowls
- Helped Green Bay score four rushing TDs in Super Bowls
- Coached Browns (1975–77), Bengals (1980–83), and Packers (1984–87)
- Acted as athletic director and coach at SMU (1988–94)

No. 55 EARL CAMPBELL

HOUSTON OILERS
NEW ORLEANS SAINTS

POSITION: RUNNING BACK
YEARS: 1978–1985
HEIGHT: 5-11 WEIGHT: 232
SCHOOL: TEXAS
HALL OF FAME: 1991

W as it the amazing Monday Night run? The unstoppable blend of speed and power? The breakaway jerseys? Or a blend of all three?

Whatever it was, Earl Campbell of the Houston Oilers gave football fans a lot to remember him by. Though his NFL career was cut short by injury at nine years, he piled up enough amazing plays in that time to create a lasting legend.

Campbell galloped into the NFL from Texas already established as a bona fide star. With the Longhorns he had won the 1977 Heisman Trophy and rushed for a stunning 1,744 yards as a senior. Not surprisingly, he was the number-one overall pick, by Houston after a trade with Tampa Bay.

All Campbell did in his first three NFL seasons was win the Rookie of the Year Award, the 1979 NFL MVP award, and a trio of rushing titles. On the way to that rookie award, he scored four touchdowns, the last on an 81-yard romp, on Monday Night Football. He ended the season as the NFL rushing leader with 1,450 yards.

The breakaway jerseys had gained him fame at Texas, the flimsy nylon peeling off in long strips, as that was about all that tacklers could grab as he rumbled by. Campbell took the style with him to the pros, and bits of light-blue fabric soon littered NFL fields. A few years after Campbell arrived, however, the league banned that type of jersey. It didn't seem to matter; tacklers still couldn't bring him down, scraps or no scraps.

In his second season, he did even better, winning another NFL rushing title with 1,697 yards while scoring a career-high 19 touchdowns. Amazingly, he improved again in his third season: Campbell's 1,934 rushing yards in 1980 was at the time the second-highest total in league history. It was the most successful three-year stint ever at the

CAREER STATS

Yrs.	Att.	Yds.	Yds./Carry	Rush TDs
8	2,187	9,407	4.3	74

start of a career. He was also named to the Pro Bowl in each of his first four seasons.

Campbell was legendarily hard to bring down. He suggested that opponents bring "five or six" guys to make the tackle. Boasting thighs that were more like tree trunks than legs, he was a threat to score on every play, as well as a threat to the self-esteem of would-be tacklers.

The pounding he took wore him down quickly, however. After racking up more than 300 carries in five of his first six seasons (and gaining 1,300 or more yards in five of those seasons), Campbell slowed down. He played the final one-and-a-half seasons with New Orleans before retiring at 30.

6 POINTS

- Four-time All-Southwest Conference at Texas
- Helped Houston reach two AFC Championship Games
- Named to five Pro Bowls
- Had NFL-record four 200-yard rushing games in 1980
- Named to NFL's All-Decade Team of 1970s
- NFL Offensive Player of the Year three consecutive seasons (1978–80)

No. 56 GENE UPSHAW

OAKLAND RAIDERS

POSITION: **GUARD**
YEARS: **1967–1981**
HEIGHT: **6-5** WEIGHT: **255**
SCHOOL: **TEXAS A&I**
HALL OF FAME: **1987**

Just because a player is a quarterback or a hard-hitting linebacker doesn't mean that other players will follow him into battle. Leadership is earned. With his punishing style of play, his total focus on winning, and his example of intense hard work, Gene Upshaw became a leader without touching the ball or making a tackle. For 15 seasons, he was the bedrock of the Oakland Raiders, who had only one losing season while he was with them.

Upshaw was enormous for a guard, towering over defensive linemen, outweighing linebackers he encountered on sweeps, and simply dwarfing unwary defensive backs. He helped the Raiders win two Super Bowls and earned selection to seven Pro Bowls.

Surprisingly, he had never played guard until he joined the Raiders. But Oakland faced off against several huge defensive tackles, notably Kansas City's Buck Buchanan, and the coaching staff wanted a big body in that guard spot. Winning the starting job as a rookie, Upshaw never left, playing 207 straight games before missing one in his final season, 1981.

Upshaw's role as a leader continued after he left the field, however. In 1983, he was hired as the director of the NFL Players' Association. In that role, he earned the same level of respect and admiration he had gained on the Raiders, forging labor deals with the league that solidified the players' positions. He held the job until his death in 2008.

6 POINTS

- NAIA All-American in college
- Oakland's No. 1 draft pick in 1967
- First-team All-Pro five times
- Only person to play in Super Bowls in three decades
- Nicknamed "Highway 63"
- Negotiated first true free agency for NFL players in 1987

MIKE SINGLETARY No. 57
CHICAGO BEARS

POSITION: LINEBACKER
YEARS: 1981–1992
HEIGHT: 6-0 **WEIGHT:** 230
SCHOOL: BAYLOR
HALL OF FAME: 1998

T he eyes had it.

While the 1985 Chicago Bears' famous "46" defense was dominating the NFL, Mike Singletary watched it all from his spot at middle linebacker. While "The Fridge" got in his spikes and the team recorded a hit single, Singletary just kept his eyes on the prize. With a pair of fumble recoveries, he got it and earned his Super Bowl ring. With that, he could finally close his eyes for a rest.

Singletary's famous scrimmage-line stare—eyes bulging, flicking side to side, seeking and, frankly, scaring—was his signature thanks to the friendly folks at NFL Films. In a dozen NFL seasons, 10 of them good enough for the Pro Bowl, Singletary created a reputation as one of the best ever at the demanding position of middle linebacker.

Some experts had thought he wouldn't be able to handle the job. At Baylor, he was a record-setting tackler, but at six feet tall, would he be big enough for the tall trees of the NFL? What he "lacked" in height, he more than made up for with study and intensity. "We're going to be here all day," he said in a famous clip.

Singletary made himself an expert in every offense he played against, acting as much as a coach on the field as a player. He exuded leadership with his play and with his constant on-field chatter. Singletary tried to bring that same intensity to his work as a head coach. It so far has proven difficult for him to get others to see the game with his piercing glare—but he'll keep at it, we're sure.

6 POINTS
- Two-time All-America at Baylor
- Made 885 solo tackles in NFL career
- Named NFL defensive player of the year for 1985 and 1988
- Won NFL Man of the Year for 1990
- Made every Pro Bowl from 1983 to 1992
- Head coach of San Francisco 49ers, 2008–2010

NO. 58 STEVE VAN BUREN

PHILADELPHIA EAGLES

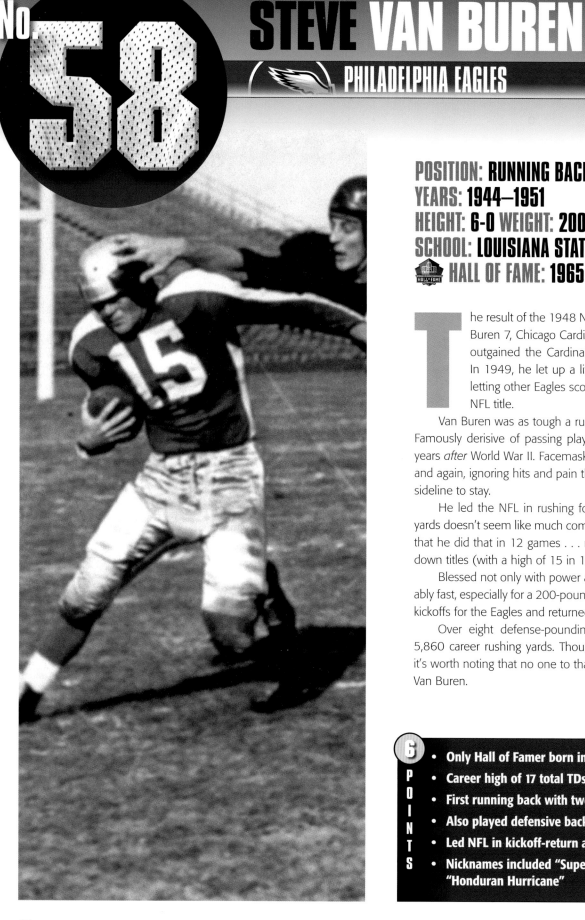

POSITION: RUNNING BACK
YEARS: 1944–1951
HEIGHT: 6-0 WEIGHT: 200
SCHOOL: LOUISIANA STATE
HALL OF FAME: 1965

The result of the 1948 NFL Championship Game? Steve Van Buren 7, Chicago Cardinals 0. On a snow-covered field, he outgained the Cardinals and scored the game's only TD. In 1949, he let up a little, only rushing for 196 yards and letting other Eagles score as they won their second straight NFL title.

Van Buren was as tough a runner as has ever played in the NFL. Famously derisive of passing plays, he played 1920s football in the years *after* World War II. Facemask-free, he plowed into the line again and again, ignoring hits and pain that would put modern backs on the sideline to stay.

He led the NFL in rushing four times. His career high of 1,146 yards doesn't seem like much compared to today's totals, but consider that he did that in 12 games . . . not 16. His four NFL rushing touchdown titles (with a high of 15 in 1945) are impressive in any era.

Blessed not only with power and toughness, he was also remarkably fast, especially for a 200-pound man. He often returned punts and kickoffs for the Eagles and returned a total of five for touchdowns.

Over eight defense-pounding seasons, Van Buren racked up 5,860 career rushing yards. Though the NFL was only 30 years old, it's worth noting that no one to that time had gained more yards than Van Buren.

6 POINTS

- Only Hall of Famer born in Honduras
- Career high of 17 total TDs in 1945 was NFL record
- First running back with two 1,000-yard seasons
- Also played defensive back and returned kicks
- Led NFL in kickoff-return average in 1945 and 1947
- Nicknames included "Supersonic Steve" and the "Honduran Hurricane"

MIKE DITKA No. 59

CHICAGO BEARS
PHILADELPHIA EAGLES
DALLAS COWBOYS

POSITION: TIGHT END
YEARS: 1961–1972
HEIGHT: 6-3 WEIGHT: 228
SCHOOL: PITTSBURGH
 **HALL OF FAME: 1988**

Most fans today know Mike Ditka as a Super Bowl–winning coach, as the personification of the tough football guy, and as a gruff TV analyst and occasional actor. But before he lived those lives, he was one of the best tight ends in the first 75 years of the NFL.

Even though Ditka was an All-America at Pitt, his rookie season with the Bears was still a huge surprise. Showing for the first time that a tight end could not only be a powerful, effective blocker—the position's main role to that time—but also a pass-catching threat, Ditka caught 56 passes, including 12 for scores. Winning the 1961 Rookie of the Year award set him on a path to record-setting greatness. His 75 catches in 1964 were the most by a tight end in the 14-game era. His career total of 427 receptions ended up second all-time at the time of his retirement.

Despite all those years of being identified with the Bears as player and coach, they were not his only NFL team. He was traded to the Eagles in 1967 and then moved to Dallas in 1969. He played his final four seasons with them and got his first Super Bowl ring near the end of his playing career. In 1971, he helped Dallas win Super Bowl VI, catching a touchdown pass in the Cowboys' 24–3 win.

Ditka moved into coaching in 1972, which led some time later to that glory year of 1985, when he pushed, prodded, and motivated "Da Bears" to a dominating Super Bowl XX championship.

6 POINTS
- Second-winningest coach in Bears history
- Career high 1,076 receiving yards in rookie season, 1961
- Made Pro Bowl each of first five seasons
- Had 43 career touchdown catches
- Head coach of Bears, 1982–1992
- Head coach of Saints, 1997–1999

No. 60 JACK HAM

 PITTSBURGH STEELERS

POSITION: LINEBACKER
YEARS: 1971–1982
HEIGHT: 6-1 **WEIGHT:** 225
SCHOOL: PENN STATE
HALL OF FAME: 1988

On a Pittsburgh Steelers team loaded with talent and personality, Jack Ham was the rock-steady glue of the Iron Curtain defense. While Mean Joe Greene did commercials and Jack Lambert scared the snot out of people, Jack Ham just did his job at outside linebacker better than pretty much anyone else. While Terry Bradshaw made jokes and Rocky Bleier inspired, Jack Ham kept going to Pro Bowl after Pro Bowl, a quiet master of his craft.

Ham came to the Steelers already a legend in his home state, having grown up in western Pennsylvania and starred for Joe Paterno at Penn State. He was a starter for the Steelers in his rookie season of 1971 and was a fixture there until he retired in 1982. It's no surprise that his career saw the emergence of the Steelers as one of the NFL's greatest dynasties, as they won four Super Bowls in six seasons. Those were the years that Ham was at his best. He earned the first of his eight straight Pro Bowls in 1973, the year before Pittsburgh won its first championship.

Ham was an expert tackler, with perfect technique and no wasted motion or energy. His pass-coverage was awesome. His coach Chuck Noll called him "the best outside linebacker I ever saw."

6 POINTS

- All-America at Penn State
- Had career-high seven picks in 1972
- Recovered 21 opponents' fumbles
- 32 career picks third most among linebackers
- Made key interception that clinched Steelers' first AFC title
- Named to NFL's 75th Anniversary All-Time Team in 1994

TOP 10 NICKNAMES

1. WILLIAM "REFRIGERATOR" PERRY

2. DICK "NIGHT TRAIN" LANE

3. "MEAN" JOE GREENE

4. WALTER "SWEETNESS" PAYTON

5. ELROY "CRAZYLEGS" HIRSCH

6. ED "TOO TALL" JONES

7. "BROADWAY" JOE NAMATH

8. REGGIE WHITE ("THE MINISTER OF DEFENSE")

9. BILLY "WHITE SHOES" JOHNSON

10. CRAIG "IRONHEAD" HEYWARD

No. 61 LADAINIAN TOMLINSON

SAN DIEGO CHARGERS
NEW YORK JETS

POSITION: RUNNING BACK
YEARS: 2001–
HEIGHT: 5-10 WEIGHT: 221
SCHOOL: TEXAS CHRISTIAN

Skip back a few spots in the NFL 100 and find Lenny Moore. The modern version is this man, LaDainian Tomlinson. Moore and others showed that a smaller, faster player—if he was also equally versatile—could be a huge part of an NFL offense; for the past 10 years, that player has been LT.

Growing up in Texas, Tomlinson modeled himself after Emmitt Smith . . . good choice for a role model. In his final season in high school, he rolled up 2,554 yards and scored 39 touchdowns. However, because he was not a "big back" in the mold that college recruiters sought—plus, he had played only one season as a starter—nearby TCU became the fallback position. Even there, he struggled for playing time. But once he got it, he showed again what he could do. In his junior year, 1999, he put together an amazing string of games: 269 yards, 300 yards, and then an NCAA-record-setting 406 yards. He led the country with 1,850 rushing yards, while scoring 18 TDs. As a senior, LT led the Horned Frogs to one of their best seasons ever, while chalking up 2,158 rushing yards, the fourth most ever in Division I.

Chosen number five overall by San Diego, Tomlinson quickly showed that he could continue his success at the highest level. His rookie-year total of 1,236 yards was the first of seven straight 1,200-yard seasons. In 2002, he set a San Diego record with 1,683 yards rushing. The numbers just kept going up. In 2003, he had 2,370 yards from scrimmage and became the first running back ever with 100 catches and more than 1,000 yards rushing in the same season.

All of these records were prelude to his 2006 season. Aided by a trio of four-touchdown games, LT set a pair of new NFL records: 28 rushing touchdowns and 31 total touchdowns. He also topped 1,200 rushing yards for the sixth year in a row. No surprise that he was named the NFL MVP.

Unfortunately for LT and the Chargers, they could never seem to win the big games when they needed to, losing in the playoffs five

CAREER STATS				
Yrs.	Att.	Yds.	Yds./Carry	Rush TDs
10	3,099	13,404	4.3	144

times, including 2006 when they had the NFL's best record at 14–2. Injuries to Tomlinson's ankle and toe slowed him enough that San Diego finally let their superstar go after the 2009 season. Joining the Jets, he found his career rejuvenated. No longer "the man," he fit in well with the Jets' team approach and has helped them reach the AFC Championship Game.

Easily the best back of the 21st century's first decade, Tomlinson's mark of 31 touchdowns might be out of reach in today's NFL.

6 POINTS

- Finished fourth in 2000 Heisman Trophy balloting
- 2,370 yards from scrimmage in 2003 fourth-most ever
- Led NFL in rushing in 2006 and 2007
- Named NFL MVP and Walter Payton Man of the Year for 2006
- Named to five Pro Bowls
- Sixth all-time (and counting) in yards from scrimmage

No. 62 RANDY WHITE

DALLAS COWBOYS

POSITION: DEFENSIVE TACKLE
YEARS: 1975–1988
HEIGHT: 6-4 WEIGHT: 257
SCHOOL: MARYLAND
HALL OF FAME: 1994

With a Lombardi Award as best lineman and an Outland Trophy as best defensive player, Randy White came to Dallas with a lot of expectations on his very large shoulders. He didn't disappoint. The player with the memorable nickname of "Manster" (half-man, half-monster) ended up making nine Pro Bowls and forging a reputation as one of the fiercest defenders of his era.

White found himself in the Super Bowl in his first season, notching a pair of sacks in the Cowboys' loss to Pittsburgh. Two years later, having moved from linebacker to defensive tackle, White really flourished. He helped Dallas reach Super Bowl XII, and his outstanding defense in that game earned him co-MVP honors, one of the handful of defensive players so honored. White and the Cowboys capped off a great run with a third NFC championship and Super Bowl appearance.

Perhaps White's greatest gift was his legendary work ethic. He missed only one game in 14 seasons and was always the last guy off the practice field. You never saw Randy White walking after a play . . . he was 100 percent, 100 percent of the time.

6 POINTS

- All-America selection at Maryland
- Selected to nine consecutive Pro Bowls
- Recovered 10 fumbles
- Had unofficial career total of 111 sacks
- Third in Cowboys' history in tackles
- Played in six NFC Championship Games and three Super Bowls

JIM OTTO No.

OAKLAND RAIDERS

POSITION: CENTER
YEARS: 1960–1974
HEIGHT: 6-2 WEIGHT: 255
SCHOOL: MIAMI (FL)
HALL OF FAME: 1980

Nothing happens on a play in football until the center snaps the ball. So you could say that Jim Otto had a hand in every Oakland Raiders offensive play during the entire history of the AFL. Otto, wearing his unique 00 jersey, was the center for the first 15 seasons of the Raiders. He joined their inaugural team in 1960 out of Miami and was a fixture until he retired in 1974. In fact, he started 210 straight games for the Raiders, never missing one due to injury.

Along the way, Otto led a famous offensive line that sent three players to the Hall of Fame—Otto, guard Gene Upshaw, and tackle Art Shell. For his part, Otto racked up honors aplenty. In the AFL's ten seasons, he was the All-AFL center every year. He added a pair of All-NFL selections after the two leagues merged in 1970. He was named to 12 Pro Bowls, too.

The Raiders struggled in their early seasons, but in the second half of Otto's career, Oakland was awesome. They won the 1967 AFL championship and played in Super Bowl II. They reeled off playoff appearances in six of Otto's final seven seasons.

You could say there will never be another Jim Otto. In a way, that's true. In 1973, the NFL changed its numbering system so that centers have to wear numbers in the 50s. No one will ever wear 00 in the NFL again. Seems only fitting . . .

6 POINTS

- One of only three players to appear in all 140 of his team's AFL games
- Named center on AFL's All-Time Team
- 210 consecutive games played is most in Raiders' history
- Third AFL player inducted into Pro Football Hall of Fame
- Elected to Pro Football Hall of Fame in first year of eligibility
- First Raider inducted into Pro Football Hall of Fame

HERB ADDERLEY

GREEN BAY PACKERS
DALLAS COWBOYS

POSITION: CORNERBACK
YEARS: 1961–1972
HEIGHT: 6-0 WEIGHT: 205
SCHOOL: MICHIGAN STATE
HALL OF FAME: 1980

Okay, NFL trivia heroes: What position did Herb Adderley play in college? If you said defensive back, go back to training camp. At Michigan State, Adderley was a running back, leading the Spartans in rushing and receptions as a senior. Arriving in the NFL in Green Bay in 1961, Adderley had a couple of guys ahead of him on the depth chart by the names of Hornung and Taylor.

However, in one of those fairy-tale switches that can sometimes lead to Canton, Adderley jumped into his old high-school role of cornerback when a Packers starter was injured. The rest, as they say, is history. Adderley thrived in the secondary for Green Bay, flying around making tackles and picking off passes—39 in his nine seasons there. He also returned kicks, taking a pair to the house. A five-time All-Pro, he was a linchpin in the Packers defense that led them to five NFL titles in the 1960s, including victories in the first two Super Bowls.

Having Adderley in the D proved to be lucky for Big D, too. After joining the Cowboys in 1970, Adderley ended up playing in four of the first six Super Bowls.

Vince Lombardi was not one to admit too many mistakes, but he owned up to almost missing out on the talent he had in the former Spartan. "When I think of what Adderley means to our defense," the great coach once said, "it scares me to think of how I almost mishandled him."

6 POINTS

- Selected as No. 1 draft pick in 1961 as a running back
- Led NFL in interception-return yardage, 1965 and 1969
- Scored three times on interception returns in 1965
- Returned 120 kickoffs, including two for touchdowns
- 60-yard TD on interception return was first in Super Bowl history
- First alphabetically among all Hall of Fame players

RANDY MOSS No. 65

MINNESOTA VIKINGS
OAKLAND RAIDERS
NEW ENGLAND PATRIOTS
TENNESSEE TITANS

POSITION: WIDE RECEIVER
YEARS: 1998–
HEIGHT: 6-4 **WEIGHT:** 215
SCHOOL: MARSHALL

The Randy Moss story will read a little differently in the future. Right now, his amazing skills and game-changing abilities are somewhat marred by a couple of rough patches in his career. But when the historians look back, they will stare in amazement at his stats and his succession of highlight-reel catches.

Moss burst into the NFL with the Vikings in 1998 and led the league with 17 TDs, the most ever by an NFL rookie receiver. His connection with strong-armed QB Randall Cunningham took Minnesota a missed field goal away from the Super Bowl. The TDs kept coming, the receiving yards piled up, and the fantasy football fans kept drooling. Opposing defenses, meanwhile, were nearly powerless to stop the tall, speedy receiver. In eight years in Minnesota, he led the NFL in TD catches three times, topped 1,300 yards in five seasons, and made the first five of his eight Pro Bowls.

The first bump in his road came after a move to Oakland that proved to be a tough fit for both team and player. He regained his superstar status with the Patriots in 2007, connecting with Tom Brady to set another NFL record with 23 touchdown catches. After another off year (for him, at least) in 2008, Moss led the NFL in TD catches for the fifth time.

His current fans might bemoan some of the issues he's given them in recent seasons, but historians will know the truth of his play. Moss was easily one of the most talented and successful receivers in NFL history.

6 POINTS

- Set rookie record with 17 touchdown catches in 1998
- Named NFL offensive rookie of the year in 1998
- Led NFL in touchdown receptions five times
- Set career highs for catches (111) and yards (1,632) in 2003
- 23 touchdown catches in 2007 is NFL single-season record
- Threw two TD passes and returned one punt for TD

No. 66 WILLIE BROWN

DENVER BRONCOS

OAKLAND RAIDERS

POSITION: **CORNERBACK**

YEARS: **1963–1978**

HEIGHT: **6-1** WEIGHT: **195**

SCHOOL: **GRAMBLING STATE**

HALL OF FAME: **1984**

Some players, even though they might have put together long and successful careers, are fixed in our collective memories for one moment. That's the case with Willie Brown. The NFL Films clip of him charging in slow-motion toward the camera, football tucked under one arm, eyes blazing, nose toward the end zone as the sunlight glints off his silver helmet, is one of the classic images of football on film.

Willie Brown set a Super Bowl record (since topped) with that 75-yard, game-winning pick in Super Bowl XI. Coming through with the big play was one of the reasons that Brown should be remembered for more than that moment. In his 16-year career, he not only redefined the idea of bump-and-run coverage, he made seven postseason interceptions, three of which he returned for scores. As proof of his big-game prowess, on 54 career regular-season picks, he scored only twice.

Brown began his career undrafted. He was cut by the Oilers and later signed with the Broncos, for whom he played his first four seasons. Joining the Raiders in 1967, it's no surprise that Oakland then went on to play in nine AFL or AFC championship games after Brown arrived to solidify the secondary. Season after season, he was the anchor of a feared Raiders' defense and the veteran counted on to shut down the other teams' top receivers.

Brown was 36 when he made that big pick against Fran Tarkenton and the Vikings. He retired in 1978, having created a legend for himself that will last far more than just a moment.

6 POINTS

- Played linebacker and tight end at Grambling State
- Undrafted, but signed then cut by Oilers
- Played in four Pro Bowls after NFL-AFL merger
- Named to All-Time All-AFL team in 1969
- Had career-high nine interceptions in 1964
- Named to NFL's All-Decade Team of 1970s

KELLEN WINSLOW No.

SAN DIEGO CHARGERS

67

POSITION: TIGHT END
YEARS: 1979–1987
HEIGHT: 6-5 WEIGHT: 251
SCHOOL: MISSOURI
HALL OF FAME: 1995

O nly a handful of NFL players' careers can be summed up in one photograph. San Diego tight end Kellen Winslow is one of those guys. He was snapped by Al Messerschmidt coming off the field after a 1981 overtime playoff game, supported on either side by teammates, spent, exhausted . . . and victorious. He had just caught 13 passes for 166 yards in the heat of Miami, then capped it all off by blocking a potentially game-winning field goal to send the game to overtime. San Diego won, 41–38.

Winslow's career was more than just one picture, but that photo is worth a thousand words. Here are just a few of them: Winslow was a key cog in the Chargers' mighty offensive machine of the 1980s. In fact, he was the first tight end to lead the NFL in receptions in 1980, his second season. He combined size, speed, and great hands in an almost-new way. Winslow was also super-tough, battling numerous knee injuries throughout his career. In fact, those injuries forced him into retirement after only nine seasons. Along the way, though, he earned five Pro Bowl selections and was named to three All-Pro teams. Along with his contemporary Ozzie Newsome, Winslow was the forerunner of the modern tight end, an all-around athletic player who contributes at the line and down the field.

That picture remains iconic in football as the picture of the warrior who gave his all. Winslow also remains as one of the best players ever at his position.

6 POINTS

- First-round pick, 13th overall, in 1979
- Career-high 10 touchdowns in 1981
- Led NFL in receptions in 1980 and 1981
- Had at least 50 catches in each of his full NFL seasons
- Personal best of 15 catches in game against Green Bay in 1984
- Tied NFL record with five receiving touchdowns in a game against Oakland in 1981

No. 68 MIKE WEBSTER

PITTSBURGH STEELERS
KANSAS CITY CHIEFS

POSITION: CENTER
YEARS: 1974–1990
HEIGHT: 6-1 **WEIGHT:** 255
SCHOOL: WISCONSIN
HALL OF FAME: 1997

Strength is the word you hear most often in stories about Mike Webster. It started with literal strength, as his powerful biceps became almost a symbol of the Steelers in the 1970s. He brought enormous physical strength to his blocking technique, first shoving around the Steelers' great defensive linemen in practice and then moving the mountains of men trying to get at his quarterback, Terry Bradshaw. Further proof came in 1980, when Webster won an offseason NFL Strongest Man contest.

But strength of will was a part of Webster, too. In one of football's toughest positions, he played 177 straight games at one point, going out finally with a dislocated elbow. In all, his 220 games are the most ever by a Pittsburgh player. With Webster as the bedrock of their offensive line, the Steelers won four Super Bowls in the 1970s, the first team to reach that total. Then there was strength of another sort: The sight of Webster in tight short sleeves in frigid December weather added to the chill felt by his opponents and to the pride felt by his teammates.

"We needed Mike," said Bradshaw when his old center went into the Hall of Fame. "He was our strength." For Bradshaw, the memories of those days of glory were still fresh on that day in Canton. After giving an introductory speech for Webster, he called for his old center to give him one more snap. Without missing a beat, Webster assumed his familiar pose . . . and the Steel Curtain rose again.

6 POINTS

- All-Big Ten center at Wisconsin
- Took over for Ray Mansfield late during 1975 season
- Selected for nine Pro Bowls
- Helped Franco Harris set career Super Bowl rushing yards record
- Once played every Steelers offensive snap for six straight years
- Started out with Kansas City as coach, ended up playing final two years there

BOBBY BELL No.

KANSAS CITY CHIEFS

69

POSITION: LINEBACKER/DEFENSIVE END
YEARS: 1963–1974
HEIGHT: 6-4 WEIGHT: 228
SCHOOL: MINNESOTA
HALL OF FAME: 1983

n football, many players are great athletes, but only when great athlete meets just the right position are superstars made. Chiefs coach Hank Stram had a hand in finding the right place for the awesome talents of Bobby Bell. Bell arrived in Kansas City after an All-America career at Minnesota as a defensive tackle. He tried defensive end first. It was not a perfect fit. But in Stram's defense, the ends sometimes dropped into coverage. On such plays, the wily Chiefs coach saw something that he would put to good use. Starting in 1965, Stram stood Bell up as an outside linebacker.

And that, as they say, was that. Bell went on to make nine AFL All-Star Games and carry the Chiefs to Super Bowls I and IV. K.C. won the latter as Bell keyed a defense that allowed Fran Tarkenton and the Vikings to score only a touchdown and gain only 67 yards on the ground.

Bell's athleticism made him perfect as a linebacker—swarming in, arms high, to block passes, or dropping into coverage to pick them off, while enjoying stuffing the run in between. He was such an all-around athlete that he acted as Kansas City's long snapper for many seasons as well. Fans remember Bell for his awesomely wide shoulders (even in a dress shirt, he looked like he was wearing shoulder pads), but opponents remember him as the guy they wanted to avoid.

6 POINTS

- Played quarterback in high school in Cleveland
- Won Outland Trophy at Minnesota (top lineman)
- Made 26 interceptions, scored six times
- Also scored on onside kick and two fumble recoveries
- Six-time first-team All-Pro
- First Kansas City Chief selected to Hall of Fame

No. 70 MARSHALL FAULK

INDIANAPOLIS COLTS
ST. LOUIS RAMS

POSITION: RUNNING BACK
YEARS: 1994–2005
HEIGHT: 5-10 WEIGHT: 211
SCHOOL: SAN DIEGO STATE
HALL OF FAME: 2011

Unprepossessing, not cut in the mold of the bruising running back, almost a guy people overlooked when he was not on the field, Marshall Faulk made sure everyone knew who he was by simply outdoing them all.

Surprisingly, he started his collegiate career as just that: overlooked. An outstanding cornerback in high school in New Orleans, he was only recruited as a running back by San Diego State. Other schools soon learned they'd made a mistake, as he set an NCAA single-game record with 386 yards as a freshman. He led the NCAA with 1,630 yards as a sophomore. He ended his three-year college career with 62 TDs, second-most all-time.

As the second overall pick of the 1994 draft, Faulk burst into the NFL with the Colts, running for 11 touchdowns and winning offensive rookie of the year honors. It was the first of his seven 1,000-yard seasons as well as the first of his six 500-yard receiving seasons. That versatility was the cornerstone of his success. Faulk had the power to carry the ball inside, the moves to make short passes into long gains, and the speed to run downfield routes.

In 1999, he became the linchpin of his new team in St. Louis, as Faulk, quarterback Kurt Warner, and the Rams piled on the points and the yards in the "Greatest Show on Turf." Guided by offensive guru Mike Martz, the team blasted through the NFL, lighting up scoreboards and frustrating defenses. The Rams, led by their dynamic duo, also led the NFL in total offense in 2000 and 2001.

"If you really want to know, that show was about three-quarters Marshall Faulk," says Warner. In fact, Faulk did set a league record for yards from scrimmage that season, rushing for 1,381 yards while catching a career-high 87 passes for 1,048 more yards. Along the way, he scored a dozen touchdowns, while providing a nearly unstoppable complement to Warner's big-game arm. The Rams beat the Titans in

CAREER STATS				
Yrs.	Att.	Yds.	Yds./Carry	Rush TDs
12	2,836	12,279	4.3	100

Super Bowl XXXIV, a thrilling contest that called on all of the Rams' weapons to succeed. The key play was a 75-yard bomb from Warner to Isaac Bruce. And though Faulk rushed for only 17 yards in that game, he caught five passes for 90 yards, including a 52-yarder.

In 2000, he led the league with 18 rushing touchdowns (plus eight more receiving), delighting Rams fans and making him one of the early darlings of the emerging fantasy-football crowd. He was named the NFL MVP that season, and added other player-of-the-year awards in 2001 with a 21-touchdown season.

Faulk's career ended after a 2005 season shortened by injury, but he had made his mark. In 2011, he was named to the Hall of Fame in his first season of eligibility.

6 POINTS

- Set NCAA freshman record with 386 yards in 1991 game
- 62 touchdowns in college was second all-time in NCAA
- Averaged NFL-high 98.7 yards per game in 2001
- Only running back with 12,000 rushing yards and 6,000 receiving yards
- 136 touchdowns was fourth-most all-time at time of retirement
- 26 TDs in 2000 was an NFL record

No. 71 PAUL WARFIELD

CLEVELAND BROWNS
MIAMI DOLPHINS

POSITION: WIDE RECEIVER
YEARS: 1964–1977
HEIGHT: 6-0 **WEIGHT:** 188
SCHOOL: OHIO STATE
HALL OF FAME: 1983

Warfield's NFL career got off to a flying start. Drafted in the first round by the Browns, he caught a career-high 52 passes (including nine for scores), helped the Browns win the NFL championship, and earned a Pro Bowl selection. Such accomplishments would become fairly regular for this supremely talented receiver.

In light of recent receivers' eye-popping stats, Warfield's career totals (427 catches, 8,565 receiving yards) are not stunning. But anyone who watched him run his precise routes and speed past defensive backs could vouch that his greatness can't be easily measured in the record book. In six years in Cleveland, he set a high standard for excellence.

Though he set career highs with 12 TD catches and 1,067 yards in 1968, he was traded to the Dolphins after the 1969 season. It was one of the biggest trades of the era. The Dolphins gave up their number-one pick in the 1970 draft, but in return they got a player who completed their championship puzzle. Two years after he joined them, the Dolphins put together their perfect season, capped off with a win in Super Bowl VII. They repeated the next year, too, with Warfield as the top pass-catcher both times.

Warfield was one of three star Dolphins players lured to the World Football League for the 1975 season, which he spent with the Memphis Southmen. The league didn't last, of course, and Warfield, ironically, spent his final two seasons back with the Browns. Receiving cognoscenti know that numbers don't tell the whole story. "No one could defend him," says one longtime NFL observer. "No one."

6 POINTS

- Miami's leader in receiving yards in each of two Super Bowl victories
- Twice named All-Pro
- Named to eight Pro Bowl teams
- Led NFL in TD catches in 1968 and 1971
- 20.1 yards-per-catch average tied for ninth all-time
- 85 career TD catches third all-time at retirement

JONATHAN OGDEN No. 72

BALTIMORE RAVENS

POSITION: TACKLE
YEARS: 1996–2007
HEIGHT: 6-9 WEIGHT: 340
SCHOOL: UCLA
HALL OF FAME ELIGIBLE IN: 2013

The Ravens needed a foundation when they were building their team from the ruins of what had been the Cleveland Browns in 1996. They chose wisely by making Ogden the first player ever chosen by the brand-new team. He moved into a starting spot at left tackle as a rookie and didn't leave for a dozen years.

How dominant was Jonathan Ogden? He played 12 NFL seasons and made the Pro Bowl in 11 of them. He was an almost unimaginable blend of mammoth size and quickness. He became one of the best pass-blocking linemen ever, and was named to the NFL's All-Decade Team for the 2000s.

Ogden and the Ravens had their biggest success in 2000, when they won their first NFL championship in Super Bowl XXXV. Though the Ravens' mighty defense earned most of the headlines, a ground-pounding offense made sure to back up the D. Leading the way was Jamal Lewis, often running behind Ogden's powerful blocking.

Ogden shared another historic season with Lewis in 2003 when the powerful back romped for 2,066 rushing yards, the second-highest single-season total ever.

Ironically, it was an injury to his toe—one of the smallest parts of his enormous frame—that led to Ogden's retirement. He was named to the Ravens' Ring of Honor and will almost certainly be headed to Canton soon.

6 POINTS

- All-America selection at UCLA
- Finished career as Ravens' all-time leader in games started
- Anchored line that allowed franchise-low 17 sacks in 2006
- Started all 16 games in seven seasons
- Has fourth-most Pro Bowl selections among offensive linemen
- Charitable foundation continues to work with Baltimore kids

TOP  10 PASS RUSHERS

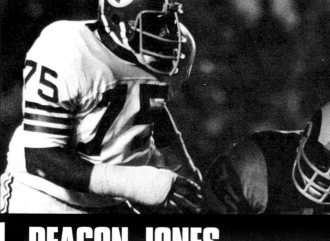

1 DEACON JONES
When you invent the word for tackling the quarterback, you get the nod as the ultimate sack-master.

2 REGGIE WHITE
One of the NFL's strongest men, in both muscle and character, White had all the moves to make him unstoppable.

3 LAWRENCE TAYLOR
Just a tackle? No. Just a running back? As if! Both together? Maaaaybe. A triple-team? Yes . . . but only sometimes.

4 BRUCE SMITH
Smith's style was a combination of overpowering strength and relentless drive.

5 GINO MARCHETTI

Tracking down QBs in opponents' backfields was nothing, since Marchetti had spent years tracking enemy soldiers.

6 KEVIN GREENE

As Greene positively flew to the quarterback, long hair streaming, fans awaited his post-sack celebrations.

7 MICHAEL STRAHAN

Did anyone ever enjoy sacking quarterbacks more? Strahan owns the single-season mark with 22.5 in 2001.

8 MARK GASTINEAU

The leading broker on the New York Sack Exchange, Gastineau's 22 sacks in 1984 was the second-most ever.

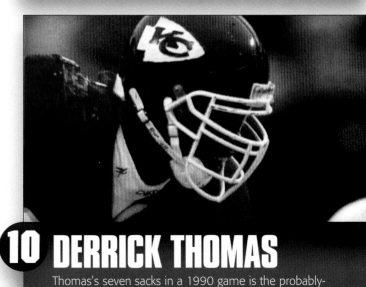

9 DOUG ATKINS

Atkins was huge (6-8), agile (a former high jump champ), and a true Bear when angered.

10 DERRICK THOMAS

Thomas's seven sacks in a 1990 game is the probably-unbeatable standard.

No. 73 OZZIE NEWSOME
CLEVELAND BROWNS

POSITION: TIGHT END
YEARS: 1978–1990
HEIGHT: 6-2 **WEIGHT:** 232
SCHOOL: ALABAMA
HALL OF FAME: 1999

No one had played tight end quite like Ozzie Newsome. With sure hands and linebacker size, Newsome put up better numbers than anyone who had ever played the position. His career totals for touchdowns, catches, and receiving yards were the standards that future star TEs such as Shannon Sharpe, Tony Gonzalez, and Antonio Gates were shooting for. It wasn't a question of breaking the mold for the position; Newsome was the one who made the mold itself.

He joined the Browns as an All-America out of Alabama in 1978 and became an instant starter. He didn't miss a game for the next 13 seasons, a streak of 198 straight that is among the best ever. Amid that streak, he created another one: catching at least one pass in 150 straight games.

Newsome played a big part in the Browns' mid-'80s success, as they advanced to three AFC Championship Games. Though Cleveland didn't reach a Super Bowl, Newsome made three trips to Hawaii for the Pro Bowl. He had six seasons with 50 or more catches as well.

Newsome was an even bigger story after he left the playing field. He was named the Ravens' general manager in 2002, becoming the first African-American to hold that post. He had been with the front office since 1996 and his moves helped the Ravens build a club that won Super Bowl XXXV and create a defense that was one of the best in the NFL in the 2000s.

6 POINTS

- Played wide receiver at Alabama
- Established Browns records with 14 receptions and 191 receiving yards against Jets in 1984
- Career highs of 1,002 yards (1981) and 89 catches (1983 and 1984)
- 47 TDs are among the most ever by a tight end
- Ravens' Vice President of Player Personnel when they won Super Bowl XXXV
- Named NFL Executive of the Year in 2000

MARION MOTLEY No. 74

CLEVELAND BROWNS
PITTSBURGH STEELERS

POSITION: FULLBACK/LINEBACKER
YEARS: 1946–1953, 1955
HEIGHT: 6-1 WEIGHT: 223
SCHOOL: NEVADA-RENO, SOUTH CAROLINA STATE
HALL OF FAME: 1968

Marion Motley broke things down. He's best known for breaking through opposing defenses as one of the most powerful and punishing runners ever. He's less well known for being one of a handful of players who were the first African-Americans in more than a quarter of a century to play pro football.

Motley had a solid college career, but had to put off his pro football dreams for several years after being called to serve in the Navy during World War II. It was on a Navy team that Paul Brown first coached the powerful back. In 1946, when Brown started the Cleveland franchise in the All-America Football Conference, Motley was one of his first players. Motley ran for more yards than anyone else in that league's four years of play. He and three other African-American players were signed by Brown for their football skills. However, they still had to put up with taunts and cheap shots from opponents who weren't ready to accept playing with black athletes.

When the Browns joined the NFL in 1950, they didn't miss a beat. Motley led the NFL with 910 yards and the Browns won the NFL title. Injuries and advancing age (he was 35 when he retired in 1955) slowed Motley down. However, he did enough in his nine professional seasons to post the highest average per carry of all time by a running back: 5.7 yards. (Note: Kansas City's Jamaal Charles is at 6.0 yards per carry through 2010, but has played six fewer seasons than Motley.) And oh, yes, he was good enough as a linebacker that Brown felt he was still Hall of Fame–caliber, even if he had concentrated on defense.

"When he ran," said Brown, "people just seemed to fly off him in every direction."

6 POINTS

- Starred for Navy's Great Lakes Naval Training Center
- Also returned kicks for three seasons
- First-team All-Pro in 1948 and 1950
- Second all-time in yards-per-carry in a game: 188 yards on 11 carries
- Motley played high school football in Canton, Ohio
- Was an exceptional blocker who allowed quarterback Otto Graham time to throw downfield

No. 75 DARRELL GREEN

WASHINGTON REDSKINS

POSITION: CORNERBACK
YEARS: 1983–2002
HEIGHT: 5-9 **WEIGHT:** 195
SCHOOL: TEXAS A&I
HALL OF FAME: 2008

For someone who was the NFL's Fastest Man for most of the 1990s, Darrell Green was a pretty good marathon runner, too. He put in 20 long years at a position demanding speed, intense concentration, and split-second timing. Toward the end of his illustrious career, he played against receivers young enough to be his sons—and at an age when normally only kickers are still on rosters. Probably the reason he has "only" 54 career interceptions is that by the time he was in his third or fourth season, opponents simply stopped throwing to his side of the field.

Green started off with a bang, returning a punt for a touchdown in his first preseason game. That same year, 1983, he scored on an interception in his first career playoff game. Fourteen years later, he became the oldest player, at 37, to record a "pick six." In fact, he had at least one interception in each of 19 seasons, an NFL record.

Green's consistent play was a big part of the Washington defense that helped the team reach three Super Bowls. He came away with Super Bowl rings for XXII and XXVI. Green was also named to seven Pro Bowls. And, of course, he famously won the NFL's Fastest Man contest four times. Thanks to all these accomplishments, Green was an easy pick for inclusion in the NFL's All-Decade Team for the 1990s.

6 POINTS

- All-America sprinter in college
- Led Redskins as rookie with 79 solo tackles
- Recovered six fumbles and returned two for touchdowns
- Longest interception return was 83 yards in 1997
- Finished career at the age of 42
- Walter Payton Man of the Year Award winner for 1996

ART SHELL No. 76

POSITION: TACKLE
YEARS: 1968–1982
HEIGHT: 6-5 WEIGHT: 268
SCHOOL: MARYLAND-EASTERN SHORE
HALL OF FAME: 1989

Other than Al Davis, no one has been a Raider for more years than Art Shell. First, he was an All-Pro tackle for 15 seasons; later, he was the team's head coach for seven more.

Shell's abilities on the offensive line were legendary. He famously kept star lineman Jim Marshall from making a single tackle when the Raiders beat Minnesota in Super Bowl XI. Future Raiders head coach Tom Flores called the game "the most perfect I've ever seen a lineman play."

A great basketball player as well as an award-winning football star, Shell joined the Raiders in 1968 and helped them reach eight AFL or AFC Championship games. Along with their victory in Super Bowl XI, Shell and the Raiders won Super Bowl XV over the Eagles. He missed just one game from 1968 to midway through the 1982 season, while both taking and meting out powerful hits game after game. Together with guard Gene Upshaw, a fellow Hall of Famer, Shell made the Raiders' offensive line the bedrock of their team. Shell was named to eight Pro Bowls.

In 1989, Davis rewarded Shell's loyalty and his football talents, promoting him to head coach, the first African-American since the early 1920s to hold such a post. Shell didn't downplay the importance of the moment, but he also didn't dwell on it. There was work to be done and games to coach . . . for the Raiders.

6 POINTS

- Selected in third round of 1968 draft
- Began career with 156 consecutive games played
- Played left tackle exclusively
- Named All-AFC six times
- Played in 23 postseason games
- Coaching career record of 58–55 with Raiders

No. 77 TONY DORSETT

DALLAS COWBOYS
DENVER BRONCOS

POSITION: RUNNING BACK
YEARS: 1977–1988
HEIGHT: 5-11 WEIGHT: 192
SCHOOL: PITTSBURGH
HALL OF FAME: 1994

Mention the name Tony Dorsett to most NFL fans, and you'll hear two things: how he pronounced his name and that amazing 99-yard run. But there are many more facts about this all-time NFL great.

Football fans got the name thing straight during his awesome college career at Pitt, which he capped off with a then-record 1,948 yards and the 1976 Heisman Trophy. He announced during his time as a Panther that he preferred to have his last name pronounced with emphasis on the second syllable: Dor-SETT. But he didn't need a name change to get attention; his game-breaking ability took care of that. Dallas thought so highly of the young runner that the Cowboys traded four draft picks for the chance to take Dorsett second overall in the 1977 draft.

The Pitt Panther made his name in the NFL quickly, gaining 1,000 yards, earning Offensive Rookie of the Year honors. It was the first of his eight 1,000-yard seasons in nine years. He wrapped up his storybook start by helping the Cowboys win Super Bowl XII. Dorsett was the leading runner in the game and scored the first touchdown in Dallas's 27–10 victory over Denver.

As he matured, Dorsett also became a talented receiver, scoring 13 career receiving touchdowns to go with his 77 rushing scores. The most famous of those touchdown runs came in a Monday-night game against Minnesota at the end of the 1982 season. Dallas had its back to its own end zone. Dorsett took a handoff at the Cowboys' one-yard line, probably just looking to get a little breathing room. He got a lot more than that. Busting through the line and then breaking a tackle at the 15, he found daylight . . . a lot of daylight. A few seconds, a great downfield block by wide receiver Drew Pearson, and 99 yards later, Dorsett had set an NFL record that can never be broken. Someone

else might run 99 yards, but you can't score a 100-yard touchdown on a play from scrimmage.

After a final season with Denver, Dorsett retired second all-time with 16,923 yards from scrimmage. Soon fans had another name to call him: Hall of Famer.

CAREER STATS				
Yrs.	Att.	Yds.	Yds./Carry	Rush TDs
12	2,936	12,739	4.3	77

6 POINTS

- First college player with at least 1,000 yards in all four seasons
- Ran for 100 or more yards 43 times
- Led NFC with 745 yards in strike-shortened 1982 season
- Threw seven-yard TD pass in 1988
- Eighth all-time with 12,739 rushing yards
- Career-high 1,646 rushing yards in 1981

BRUCE MATTHEWS

HOUSTON OILERS/TENNESSEE TITANS

POSITION: GUARD/CENTER/TACKLE
YEARS: 1983–2001
HEIGHT: 6-5 **WEIGHT:** 305
SCHOOL: SOUTHERN CALIFORNIA
 **HALL OF FAME:** 2007

Offensive linemen usually specialize. They play one position well, and usually even just one side of the ball (left or right). Bruce Matthews tossed that notion out the window, playing every one of the five line positions and earning Pro Bowl selections at guard and center. He was named to his first Pro Bowl in 1988 and didn't miss another, a record-tying streak of 14 straight trips to Hawaii.

Along with his versatility, Matthews is remembered for his longevity. When he finally retired in 2001, he had played in 296 regular-season and 15 postseason games. No non-kicker to that point had played in as many NFL games. How long did Matthews end up sticking around? In 1994, the Oilers made Jeff Fisher their head coach. Fisher and Matthews had been teammates at USC!

Matthews came by his football longevity genetically. His father was a lineman with the 49ers, and his brother Clay played linebacker for 16 years for the Browns and Falcons.

Steady, strong, and supremely gifted at the task of blocking just about anything, Matthews earned nine spots on the All-Pro team and was named to the NFL's All-Decade Team for the 1990s. The only tricky part there was which position: the selectors settled on guard, the position Matthews played most often.

6 POINTS

- First-team All-Pro nine times
- Tied Merlin Olsen for most consecutive Pro Bowl selections (14)
- Started 99 games at left guard, 67 at right guard, 87 at center, 22 at right tackle, and 17 at left tackle
- Named NFL Lineman of the Year three times
- Played in Super Bowl XXXIV loss to Rams
- Nephew Clay Matthews III stars at LB for Green Bay Packers

EMLEN TUNNELL No.79

NEW YORK GIANTS
GREEN BAY PACKERS

POSITION: DEFENSIVE BACK
YEARS: 1948–1961
HEIGHT: 6-1 WEIGHT: 187
SCHOOL: IOWA/TOLEDO
HALL OF FAME: 1967

The Giants ran something they called the Umbrella Defense for most of the 1950s (it must have worked pretty well; they played in three NFL Championship Games and won it all in 1956). At the top of the umbrella, the last line of defense, they needed a player with speed, strength, and the ability to react instantly to whatever danger occurred. In a former Coast Guardsman who showed up on their doorstep asking for a job, they found their man.

Emlen Tunnell had played on and off for Iowa and Toledo on either side of serving in the Coast Guard. In 1948, he decided to move to the pros, and asked the Giants for a job. He became the first African-American to play for the Giants and was soon the best in the league at defensive back.

He had at least seven interceptions in each of his first ten seasons, with a career high of 10 in 1949. He continued as a ferocious ballhawk throughout his 14-year career (Giants coaches called him "offense on defense"), ending with a then-record 79 picks. Tunnell's 1,282 return yards were also a record, though since topped by several players.

Tunnell was also a great punt returner, twice leading the league in return yards and scoring five career punt-return touchdowns.

He played with the Packers for his final three seasons, helping Green Bay win its first NFL title in his final season, 1961. In 1967, Tunnell became the first African-American player—and the first player who was almost exclusively on defense—chosen for the Hall of Fame.

6 POINTS

- Was turned down by Army and Navy due to college neck injury
- All-NFL six seasons
- Scored only kickoff-return TD in 1951
- Missed only one Pro Bowl in the 1950s
- Carried four interceptions back for scores
- Named as safety on All-Time Team for 1969

No. 80 TROY AIKMAN

DALLAS COWBOYS

POSITION: QUARTERBACK
YEARS: 1989–2000
HEIGHT: 6-4 WEIGHT: 219
SCHOOL: OKLAHOMA/UCLA
HALL OF FAME: 2006

After spending most of his youth in Oklahoma, California-born Troy Aikman thought his dream had come true when he headed off to play quarterback for the Sooners. But things didn't work out at Oklahoma, and he moved to UCLA, where all he did was have one of the best college careers of the past 50 years.

Learning how to bounce back came in handy after Aikman moved to the NFL. He was chosen by Dallas with the first overall pick of the 1989 draft. In his first season as the Cowboys' starter, the team had a less-than-sterling 1–15 record, including 0–11 in Aikman's starts. But as he had with his college situation, he stuck with it and kept working. The next year, the Cowboys won seven games and Aikman topped 2,500 passing yards. A year later, they were in the playoffs.

Aikman's quiet leadership, strong, accurate arm, and country-boy toughness were a perfect fit in the Cowboys' offense of the 1990s. With a one-two punch of Emmitt Smith and Michael Irvin, Aikman had some powerful weapons. In 1992, the team went 13–3, eventually trouncing Buffalo 52–17 in Super Bowl XXVII. Aikman had four touchdown passes and was named the Super Bowl MVP.

That season was the first of a four-year dynasty (1992–95) that was one of the most dominant in NFL history. The Cowboys won three of four Super Bowls, and Aikman's pinpoint passing was a huge part of their success. He was calm and cool, even when dealing with some of the Cowboys' more fiery personalities, both players and coaches. His leadership came by example, rather than rah-rah. With 90 wins in the 1990s, Aikman set a record (since broken by Peyton Manning) for wins in a decade.

Aikman's fearlessness eventually proved his undoing. A series of major hits forced him to retire with concussion-related issues. With three Super Bowl rings, he was an easy pick for the Hall of Fame in his first year of eligibility.

Aikman has since become a respected analyst, bringing the experience of one of the best QBs of the past quarter-century to the broadcast booth.

CAREER STATS

Yrs.	W-L	Yds.	TD	Rating
12	94-71	32,942	165	81.6

6 POINTS

- Had career-high 23 TD passes in 1992
- Led NFL with 69.1 completion percentage in 1993
- Career playoff record of 11–4
- Named to six Pro Bowls
- Won Walter Payton Man of the Year Award for 1997
- Returned to school in 2009 to complete UCLA degree

TOP 10 CLUTCH QUARTERBACKS

1 JOE MONTANA
When the game was at its most intense, Montana seemed to be the most relaxed person in the stadium.

2 JOHN ELWAY
They called it "Elway Magic." Whatever it was, he waved his wand and led Denver to dozens of come-from-behind wins.

3 TOM BRADY
Brady won the Pats' first two Super Bowls with clutch performance on nail-biting, late-game drives.

4 ROGER STAUBACH
The inventor of the "Hail Mary" pass, Staubach fought like the Navy man he was: Never give up the ship.

5 JOHN UNITAS

If you invent the two-minute drill, as Unitas did, you deserve a place on this list.

6 KEN STABLER

"The Snake" never gave up, no matter how late the game or desperate the situation, and led with fire and heart.

7 OTTO GRAHAM

Ten times, Graham's teams needed him to lead them to victory for a chance at the title. Ten times, he came through.

8 BART STARR

His game-winning Ice Bowl sneak was just one of a dozen or more examples of Starr doing what it took to win.

9 STEVE YOUNG

Young could win late games with his arm or with his legs, but when he used his heart, he was truly clutch.

10 DAN MARINO

Marino was like a gunslinger who always had one more bullet on his belt . . . ready to strike for the final victory.

No. 81

STEVE YOUNG

TAMPA BAY BUCCANEERS
SAN FRANCISCO 49ERS

POSITION: QUARTERBACK
YEARS: 1985–1999
HEIGHT: 6-2 WEIGHT: 215
SCHOOL: BRIGHAM YOUNG
HALL OF FAME: 2005

I t's one thing to be really, really good at something. Steve Young was that as a passer, setting NCAA records at BYU and then throwing laser beams as a pro, first in the USFL and then the NFL. In fact, he led the NFL in passing a record-tying six times. His 112.8 rating in 1994 was the highest ever recorded to that time. (His career passer rating of 96.8 is still third all-time.)

It's entirely another to be really, really good at something else *as well*. Young was one of the best running QBs ever, scoring a then-record 43 touchdowns on the ground while often outgaining his running backs and frustrating would-be sackers.

Oh, and then it turns out he's not only really, really good at all of those things, but he also won games, is a terrific TV analyst, and is darned good-looking. It's just not fair.

But for all his skills and all the successes he racked up, Young was his team's full-time starter only one year out of his first six in the NFL.

After his All-America senior season at BYU, Young was one of the stars lured by USFL money to try to kickstart that new league when it began in 1982. After a couple seasons of being chased by defenders who were quicker than his linemen, but usually not quicker than he was, Young was chosen by the Buccaneers in a supplemental draft of USFL alumni. After a few mostly uneventful years in Tampa Bay, Young was traded to the 49ers. Unfortunately for Young, a guy named Montana (see #4 on this list) was already installed as San Francisco's QB. Young bided his time, learning from the master, until he got his chance to take over in 1991.

It was worth the wait for Niners fans, who watched Young lead San Francisco to seven straight winning seasons. The high point came in Super Bowl XXIX after the 1994 season. While setting a title-game record with six touchdown passes, Young led the Niners to a numerically appropriate 49–26 win over San Diego. And how fitting for the

CAREER STATS

Yrs.	W-L	Yds.	TD	Rating
15	94-49	33,124	232	96.8

do-everything QB that he was the game's leading rusher with, that's right, 49 yards.

Young retired after playing three games in the 1999 season, moving easily into a role on TV, where his QB smarts and easy manner have made him a regular on ESPN.

No. 82 TED HENDRICKS

BALTIMORE COLTS
GREEN BAY PACKERS
OAKLAND RAIDERS

POSITION: LINEBACKER
YEARS: 1969–1983
HEIGHT: 6-7 WEIGHT: 220
SCHOOL: MIAMI (FL)
HALL OF FAME: 1990

Wherever the Mad Stork landed, he was a star. At the University of Miami, Ted Hendricks, who at 6-7 got his famous nickname thanks to his imposing wingspan, was a three-time All-America. In five years with the Baltimore Colts, he was an All-Pro and helped the Colts win Super Bowl V. He only played one year (1974) in Green Bay, but in that time he picked off five passes, blocked seven kicks, and earned another All-Pro nod.

Amazingly, the Packers let Hendricks go after that one stunning season. In his seventh year in the NFL, Hendricks finally found his true home with the Raiders. His all-out style and personality meshed perfectly with the Raiders' way of playing, and he was a huge part of their devastating defense of the late 1970s and early 1980s. Along with using his massive size to overwhelm blockers and clog running lanes, he used his imposing height to block 25 kicks in his career. Though official records of such things are not kept, it is thought that the Stork's is the highest total ever.

Along with his disruptive ability on the field, in Oakland Hendricks found a place for his buoyant, offbeat personality. From riding a horse onto a practice field to showing up with a pumpkin for a helmet, Hendricks exhibited a truly unique style. But though he got laughs for his odd ways, he earned respect for his hard-nosed play. Despite facing constant contact as a linebacker, Hendricks ended his career with a streak of 215 straight games. The final one gave him his fourth Super Bowl ring, as he helped the Raiders trounce Washington in Super Bowl XVIII. And then the Stork flew off into the sunset . . .

6 POINTS

- Also played defensive end at Miami
- Four career NFL safeties are tied for most ever
- Picked off 26 passes and recovered 16 fumbles
- Scored two touchdowns in NFL career
- Only Hall of Fame player born in Guatemala
- Selected to eight Pro Bowls

NORM VAN BROCKLIN No.

LOS ANGELES RAMS
PHILADELPHIA EAGLES

83

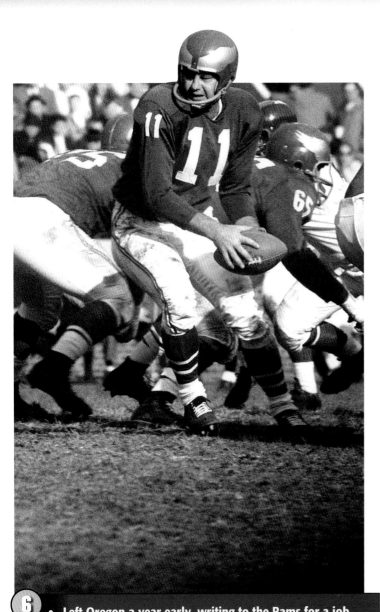

POSITION: QUARTERBACK
YEARS: 1949–1960
HEIGHT: 6-1 WEIGHT: 190
SCHOOL: OREGON
 **HALL OF FAME: 1971**

How's this for a tough spot? In 1950, Norm Van Brocklin won the NFL passing title. In 1951, he set an all-time record with 554 yards passing in a single game. That season, he also led the Rams to the NFL title, clinching it with a 73-yard TD pass to Tom Fears in the championship game. In 1952, he won every game he started.

What was so tough about that? The Dutchman, as he was known, didn't even start every game for the Rams! When he joined the team in 1949, they already had an all-star QB, Bob Waterfield. The two shared starting duties through 1952, each of them leading the league in various passing categories even though neither played a full season. The famously hard-nosed Van Brocklin chafed in the two-fer situation. After Waterfield left, Dutch finally took over the team and led them to three straight winning seasons. Then the Rams brought in Billy Wade and created yet another controversy. Van Brocklin had had enough. He retired after the 1957 season.

The Eagles recognized greatness, however, and lured him back. By 1960, he had carried them to the NFL championship. He was named the league's Most Outstanding Player and then retired again . . . this time for good, the master of his own fate.

Speaking of tough, few quarterbacks both earned and deserved a reputation for toughness on the field. His take-no-prisoners style earned him the respect of both teammates and defenders alike.

6 POINTS

- Left Oregon a year early, writing to the Rams for a job
- Scored a total of 11 rushing TDs
- Led NFL with 2,637 passing yards in 1954
- Led NFL in passer rating in 1950 and 1952
- Was also his teams' punter each season, averaging nearly 43 yards per punt
- Later was NFL head coach for 13 seasons

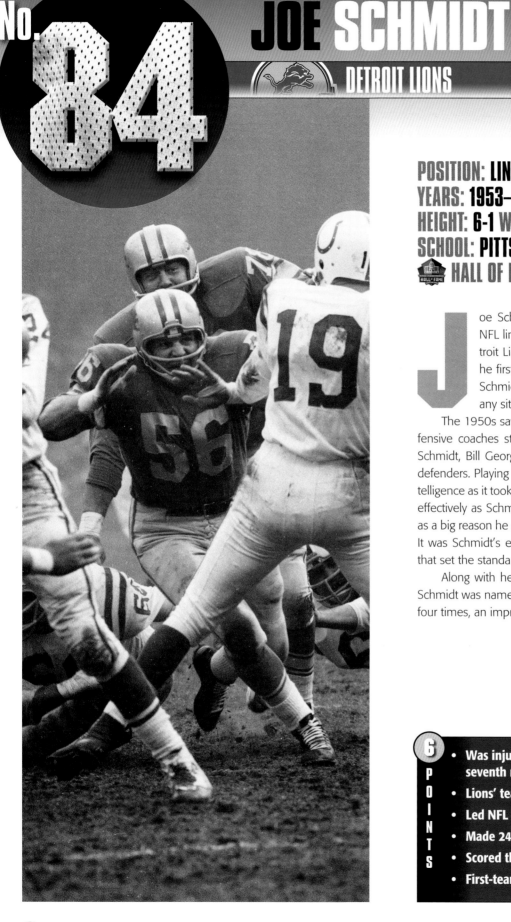

No. 84

JOE SCHMIDT

DETROIT LIONS

POSITION: LINEBACKER
YEARS: 1953–1965
HEIGHT: 6-1 WEIGHT: 220
SCHOOL: PITTSBURGH
HALL OF FAME: 1973

Joe Schmidt was so unassuming and built so unlike an NFL linebacker that the man who drafted him for the Detroit Lions thought he was just another college kid when he first met him. As his 13-year NFL career would prove, Schmidt was not a boy among men, but a mighty man in any situation.

The 1950s saw a real flowering of the position of linebacker. Defensive coaches started using powerful but athletic players such as Schmidt, Bill George, and Sam Huff as both run-stoppers and pass-defenders. Playing the position well took as much preparation and intelligence as it took physical skills. Few players combined those traits as effectively as Schmidt. Teammates pointed to his intense preparation as a big reason he seemed to be able to sense what was coming next. It was Schmidt's example of being a sort of "defensive quarterback" that set the standard for middle linebackers in the years ahead.

Along with helping the Lions win a pair of NFL championships, Schmidt was named to ten straight Pro Bowls and was the Lions' MVP four times, an impressive feat for a defensive player.

6 POINTS
- Was injured a lot in college, so was not selected until seventh round
- Lions' team captain for nine seasons
- Led NFL with eight fumble recoveries in 1955
- Made 24 career interceptions
- Scored three career defensive touchdowns
- First-team All-Pro eight times

MARCUS ALLEN No. 85

LOS ANGELES RAIDERS
KANSAS CITY CHIEFS

POSITION: RUNNING BACK
YEARS: 1982–1997
HEIGHT: 6-2 WEIGHT: 210
SCHOOL: SOUTHERN CALIFORNIA
 **HALL OF FAME: 2003**

Marcus Allen was the epitome of style as a runner. Speedy, smooth, and deceptively tough, he seemed to glide through defenses rather than run through or around them. Though he topped 1,000 rushing yards in only three of his 16 NFL seasons, he is still in the top 15 all-time with 12,243 yards—a testament to his steady production. Another hallmark of his career was his versatility; his 1985 total of 2,314 yards from scrimmage was an all-time best until topped by Barry Sanders in 1997. (Note: Chris Johnson holds the mark now: 2,509 yards in 2009.) At the time of his retirement in 1997, Allen was also the NFL's all-time leader in rushing touchdowns.

Allen was a superstar at USC, winning the Heisman Trophy in 1981. He wasted no time in making his mark on the NFL, leading the league with 11 rushing touchdowns and being named Offensive Rookie of the Year for 1982. He had his best overall season in 1985, earning NFL MVP honors while setting that yards from scrimmage record and also leading the NFL with 1,759 rushing yards.

His most famous run came in Super Bowl XVIII. In the midst of the Raiders' 38-9 shellacking of the Redskins, Allen took a handoff in the third quarter, reversed field, threaded back through the line, and then found open field. Seventy-four yards later, he had set a record (since topped) for longest TD run in the Super Bowl.

Allen left the Raiders in 1992 after a dispute with Al Davis, but flourished with his new team, the Chiefs. He was named to another Pro Bowl and led the NFL with 12 touchdowns in 1993.

The all-time great was a shoo-in for the Hall of Fame in his first year of eligibility.

6 POINTS

- First player in NFL history with 10,000 rushing and 5,000 receiving yards
- Named MVP of Super Bowl XVIII
- Scored at least 11 touchdowns in seven different seasons
- 587 career receptions ranks fourth all-time among running backs
- Scored 47 touchdowns in five seasons with Chiefs
- Gained at least 1,000 yards from scrimmage 11 times

No. 86 WILLIE DAVIS

 CLEVELAND BROWNS
GREEN BAY PACKERS

POSITION: DEFENSIVE END/DEFENSIVE TACKLE
YEARS: 1958–1969
HEIGHT: 6-3 **WEIGHT:** 243
SCHOOL: GRAMBLING STATE
HALL OF FAME: 1981

At the beginning of his third NFL season, Willie Davis found himself on a new team and playing a new full-time position. And he was doing it all for Vince Lombardi. For many players, that would have been too much to handle. For Davis, it was just what he wanted.

A multi-position lineman at Grambling State, Davis spent his first two NFL seasons (after two seasons playing on Uncle Sam's team in the Army) with the Browns shuttling between offense and defense and not really settling in. In a trade that ranks as one of the dumbest in NFL history, the Browns sent Davis to Green Bay for a receiver who would make one catch in Cleveland. Davis, meanwhile, was given his marching orders by Lombardi: You're a defensive end. Go to town.

"That was what I wanted to hear," Davis said. "I thought I was better suited for defense. I played with a certain frenzy."

On a team studded with stars, Davis stood out for his tenacity at the point of attack. His hallmarks were his speed and his ability to sense the opponent's play. He seemed like he was always in the right place at the right time.

Davis was part of all five of the Packers' NFL championships in the 1960s and helped them win the first two Super Bowls. In Super Bowl II, he had three sacks. A five-time Pro Bowl performer, Davis didn't get as much ink as the Nitschkes, Starrs, and Taylors in Green Bay, but he was as big a part of their title run as anyone.

6 POINTS

- 181st overall pick of 1956 NFL Draft
- First-team All-Pro five times
- Recovered Packers-record 21 fumbles in his career
- Registered two career safeties
- Did not miss a game in his 12-year career
- In two Super Bowls, unofficially registered 4.5 sacks

CRAZYLEGS HIRSCH No. 87

LOS ANGELES RAMS

POSITION: WIDE RECEIVER
YEARS: 1946–1957
HEIGHT: 6-2 WEIGHT: 190
SCHOOL: WISCONSIN/MICHIGAN
HALL OF FAME: 1968

He'd be famous enough for having one of the most colorful and descriptive nicknames in NFL history, but Elroy "Crazylegs" Hirsch earned his rep for his play before he went down in history for his moniker.

Looking at his career stats in a vacuum, you'd wonder why he was named the best flanker ever in a 1969 poll to name the NFL's 50th Anniversary All-Time Team. After all, his 387 catches in 12 pro seasons would have been *three* good years for someone like Cris Carter. But it was not so much the raw numbers that made Hirsch so outstanding, it was the style in which he put them up. The combination of his downfield speed and nickname-inspiring running form made him the greatest long-ball threat of the game's first half-century. In 1951, when he caught an NFL-record-tying 17 touchdowns, 10 of them went for 40 or more yards. For two seasons running, he averaged nearly 23 yards per catch. Though the pass was certainly a bigger part of the sport than it had been in previous decades, it was Hirsch and a select few others who created the "vertical" passing game.

Hirsch was an All-America running back at Michigan and signed with the fledgling All-America Football Conference in 1946. After three self-proclaimed "frightful" years with the Chicago Rockets, he joined the Rams and set about becoming a star. Teaming with strong-armed passers Bob Waterfield and Norm Van Brocklin, Hirsch blossomed, reaching his peak in 1951 with those record TDs as well as league-leading totals of 66 catches and 1,495 receiving yards. He played with the Rams through 1957, earning three Pro Bowl selections and continuing to stretch defenses. Crazylegs set the stage for the present use of speed in modern passing offenses.

6 POINTS

- His 1,495 receiving yards in 1951 was an NFL record
- All-America at Wisconsin before transferring to Michigan
- Led NFL in scoring in 1951 with 102 points
- His 124.6 yards per game average in 1951 was a record until 1982
- His 17 TD catches in 1951 weren't topped until 1984
- Also played defensive back occasionally; had 15 career interceptions

No. 88 ED REED

BALTIMORE RAVENS

POSITION: SAFETY
YEARS: 2002–
HEIGHT: 5-11 WEIGHT: 220
SCHOOL: MIAMI (FL)

R eed came to the NFL with a big rep, earned with a great career at Miami. He capped it off with an All-America season as a senior, helping the Hurricanes win the national championship. One publication even named him its player of the year—among all players, not just defenders.

Since he jumped into a starting role as a rookie in 2002, Reed has more than lived up to expectations. You want consistent? Reed has had at least five picks in seven of his nine NFL seasons. He had returned six of them for TDs through 2010. You want admired? He has earned seven Pro Bowl selections and was named to the NFL's All-Decade Team for the 2000s. You want contributions on the scoreboard? Reed has 12 TDs and is the only player in NFL history to score on all four of these plays: returns of a punt, a blocked punt, a fumble, and an interception. You want leadership? He has led the NFL in pick-offs three times (2004, 2008, and 2010). You want excitement? Two of his returns are the longest in NFL history: 106 yards in 2004 and 107 yards in 2008.

You'd think that after a while teams would stop throwing his way, but a big part of Reed's genius on the field is that he overcomes his own success. Even though offenses are geared to avoid him, he finds a way to be disruptive.

Reed's best individual season came in 2004 when he set career highs with nine interceptions and 358 return yards, while adding 89 tackles and a pair of sacks.

His multi-faceted game has set a new standard for safeties in the NFL.

6 POINTS

- Broke 43-year-old NFL record with 358 interception-return yards in 2004

- Returned three blocked kicks for touchdowns

- Occasionally returns punts, including one for TD in 2007

- Has added five sacks to his stats

- Career interception return average of 26.6 is best all-time

- Charitable foundation is active with kids in Baltimore and New Orleans

ERNIE NEVERS No. 89

DULUTH ESKIMOS
CHICAGO CARDINALS

POSITION: HALFBACK/DEFENSIVE BACK/KICKER
YEARS: 1926–1927, 1929–1931
HEIGHT: 6-0 WEIGHT: 204
SCHOOL: STANFORD
HALL OF FAME: 1963

Ernie Nevers was one of the most talented athletes to play in the early years of the NFL . . . and one of the best. He's most remembered by NFL fans for one amazing day in 1929. Playing for the Chicago Cardinals against the Chicago Bears, Nevers scored six touchdowns and kicked four extra points. His one-man-team total of 40 remains a single-game record. That was all the points the Cardinals scored in the game as well. The next week, he was a one-man show again, though he slacked off with only 19 points.

Success on any field was no surprise to anyone who had watched this all-around star. No less a visionary than Pop Warner, his coach at Stanford, called Nevers "the football player without a fault." Nevers actually went another way after Stanford, first joining the American League's St. Louis Browns to pitch. He spent parts of three seasons on the diamond, giving up a pair of homers to Babe Ruth in 1927, while spending his fall weekends playing football.

Actually, in 1926, he spent more than just weekends. The Eskimos were a team without a home field. They were always on the road. Along with 14 "official" NFL games, the team played a dozen or so exhibitions. Nevers didn't miss a game on offense or defense. He was a do-everything player in a two-way era, playing halfback, defensive back, and kicker.

All that hard work caused injuries that kept him off the football field (but not the diamond) in 1928, but he came back in 1929 with the Cardinals, acting as player-coach in 1930 and 1931. Nevers then left behind his athletic life, but not without a final appearance in an all-star game played for charity. No surprise here: He scored all 26 of his team's points.

6 POINTS

- Gained fame by playing on newly healed ankles in 1925 Rose Bowl
- First pro contract for $15,000 was one of the largest ever at the time
- Kicker and punter for most teams he played for
- Named first-team All-Pro in all five of his NFL seasons
- Charter enshrinee into Pro Football Hall of Fame
- His 40-point game in 1929 is the NFL's longest-standing individual record

No. 90 KURT WARNER

ST. LOUIS RAMS
NEW YORK GIANTS
ARIZONA CARDINALS

POSITION: QUARTERBACK
YEARS: 1998–2009
HEIGHT: 6-2 **WEIGHT:** 220
SCHOOL: NORTHERN IOWA
HALL OF FAME ELIGIBLE IN: 2015

CAREER STATS				
Yrs.	W-L	Yds.	TD	Rating
12	67-49	32,344	208	93.7

When Kurt Warner looked into the cameras after winning Super Bowl XXXIV and said, "I'm going to Disney World!" it was old hat. After all, he'd already lived out one of the greatest fairy tales in sports history.

Warner and the Rams' "Greatest Show on Turf" had just survived a furious comeback by the Tennessee Titans. Warner had created the winning points with a 73-yard bomb to Isaac Bruce with just over two minutes left in what was then a tie game. It was the latest and most important salvo from the right arm of a guy who famously had been stuffing grocery bags just a few years earlier.

How Warner arrived at the pinnacle of NFL success and became a national hero was one of the wildest stories in recent NFL annals. Undrafted out of Northern Iowa, he was working at a grocery store when he signed on with the indoor-football Iowa Barnstormers. There, he caught the eye of officials stocking NFL Europe teams and so the grocery bagger headed to Amsterdam to play for the Admirals.

Success overseas led to his signing with the Rams in 1998 and being handed the reins of Mike Martz's high-powered offense. After a preseason injury the following season to Trent Green, Warner's powerful, accurate arm and ability to hang tough against the rush were a perfect fit. The 1999 Rams poured on the points and Americans loved the story of the grocery-store clerk heading to the Super Bowl. When he walked away with the game's MVP award (and that trip to Disney World), Warner's place in NFL folklore was assured.

Just four years after his Super Bowl triumph, however, he was gone from St. Louis, the victim of injuries and the emergence of Marc Bulger. But this football Cinderella story had another chapter. Warner landed in Arizona after a humbling year with the Giants. In his fourth season in the desert, still firing rockets at 37 years old, he led the upstart Cardinals to their first Super Bowl berth. Though they had won only nine games in the regular season, they beat three "better" teams in the playoffs and then stared down the Steelers in Super Bowl XLIII. Warner's magic ran headlong into a magical grab by Santonio Holmes in the final seconds, and Arizona lost 27–23. Even though he lost, for Warner, it was another heart-warming tale in this football fantasy.

He played one more season and then hung up his cleats, heading home to a life almost as busy as that of an NFL quarterback—father of a brood of seven.

- Guided two Iowa Barnstormers teams to Arena Bowl championship games
- Career 66.5 completion percentage is second all-time
- Named NFL MVP for 1999 and 2001
- Named to Pro Bowl in 1999, 2000, 2001, and 2008
- Spent 2004 with Giants, starting nine games
- Career postseason record of 9–4

TOP 10 JERSEY NUMBERS

1 **#12** Tom Brady, Jim Kelly, Terry Bradshaw, Aaron Rodgers, Randall Cunningham, John Brodie, Rich Gannon, Roger Staubach, Joe Namath, Ken Stabler

2 **#32** Jim Brown, O.J. Simpson, Marcus Allen, Franco Harris, Ricky Watters

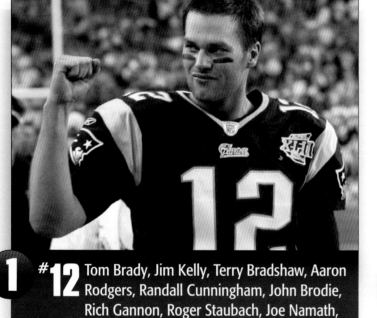

3 **#80** Jerry Rice, Cris Carter, Isaac Bruce, Donald Driver, Rod Smith, Andre Johnson, Steve Largent, James Lofton, Kellen Winslow

4 **#34** Walter Payton, Earl Campbell, Ricky Williams, Bo Jackson, Herschel Walker, Thurman Thomas

5 **#21** Deion Sanders, Tiki Barber, LaDainian Tomlinson, Charles Woodson, Frank Gore, Cliff Branch

6 **#20** Barry Sanders, Brian Dawkins, Billy Simms

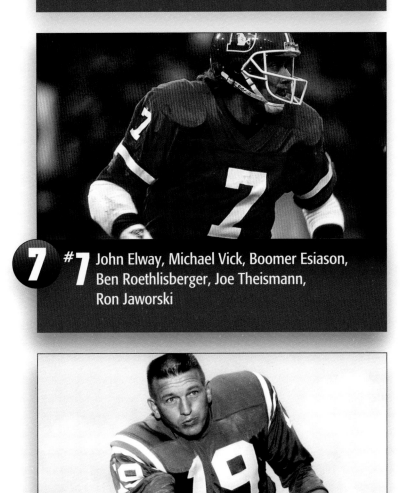

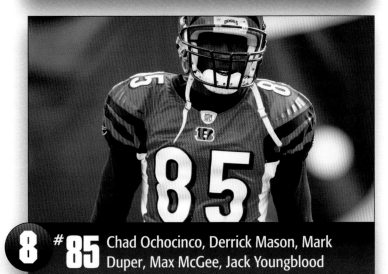

7 **#7** John Elway, Michael Vick, Boomer Esiason, Ben Roethlisberger, Joe Theismann, Ron Jaworski

8 **#85** Chad Ochocinco, Derrick Mason, Mark Duper, Max McGee, Jack Youngblood

9 **#19** Johnny Unitas, Lance Alworth, Bernie Kosar

10 **#99** Warren Sapp, Jerome Brown, Jason Taylor, Dan Hampton, Mark Gastineau

No. 91

FRAN TARKENTON

MINNESOTA VIKINGS
NEW YORK GIANTS

POSITION: QUARTERBACK
YEARS: 1961–1978
HEIGHT: 6-0 WEIGHT: 180
SCHOOL: GEORGIA
HALL OF FAME: 1986

CAREER STATS				
Yrs.	W-L	Yds.	TD	Rating
18	124-109-6	47,003	342	80.4

If most quarterbacks of his era were tall trees, Fran Tarkenton was a scrambling sapling. Only six feet tall on a good day and allegedly 180 pounds, Tarkenton nevertheless was one of the most consistently successful passers of all time. He was in the top three in passing yards in the NFL in 10 different seasons and passing TDs in nine seasons. But throwing the ball was not what he was best known for. Instead, "Scramblin' Fran" remains one of the most elusive, hard-to-catch QBs ever, a constant source of frustration for every defensive player who ever got tired just chasing him in, around, and out of the pocket.

His career got off to a hot start. In the first-ever Minnesota Vikings game, he relieved starter George Shaw and threw four touchdown passes. He also scored the first of his 32 career rushing TDs (a total that is still among the most ever by a quarterback) and the Vikings pulled off a shocking 37–13 upset of the venerable Chicago Bears. By the end of the season, he was firmly entrenched as the starter. However, as good as he was, he was not surrounded by NFL finery, and the Vikings had only one winning record in his first six seasons. Before the 1967 season, Minnesota shocked its fans by sending Tark to the Giants for four draft choices. In New York, Tarkenton mellowed some of his elusive ways, throwing for career highs in yards and touchdowns in that first year.

However, after five seasons (and four of his nine Pro Bowl selections) in New York, Tarkenton was in the middle of another surprising trade—back home to the Vikings. Though he was moving into his mid-30s, he had the best seasons of his career, leading the Vikings to three Super Bowls (after the 1973, 1974, and 1976 seasons) and leading the NFL in completions three times. He was also the NFL MVP in 1975. Though he could never bring them the ultimate prize, it was his leadership and do-what-it-takes style that made the Vikings offense go.

After the 1978 season, he went out on top, having led the league and set career highs in completions, attempts, and yards at the age of 38. Tarkenton proved he was not just a scrambler. At his retirement, the "little guy" stood tall. At that point, Tarkenton was the all-time NFL leader in attempts, completions, passing yards, and touchdown passes. Though all those marks have since been topped, it turned out that, in the end, the only way they caught Tarkenton was because he finally just stopped running.

6

POINTS

- Selected in third round by Vikings in 1961
- First player to reach 47,000 passing yards (47,003)
- 342 TD passes now fourth all-time
- Rushed for at least 300 yards in seven seasons
- Led Vikings to six NFC Central titles
- Post-playing career work included being a broadcaster on Monday Night Football

No. 92 MICHAEL IRVIN

DALLAS COWBOYS

POSITION: WIDE RECEIVER
YEARS: 1988–1999
HEIGHT: 6-2 WEIGHT: 207
SCHOOL: MIAMI (FL)
HALL OF FAME: 2007

After lighting up college scoreboards in an All-America career at high-flying Miami, Michael Irvin came crashing down to earth when he joined the then-lowly Dallas Cowboys in 1988. He showed flashes of his collegiate skills and perhaps hinted at the greatness ahead, but his first three pro seasons were mostly forgettable.

Then came 1991, the full flourishing of quarterback Troy Aikman, and the start of one of the most remarkable runs ever by a team. Irvin's pass-catching skills were a vital component of a Cowboys offense that would yee-haw its way to three Super Bowl titles in four seasons (1992–95). Irvin went from 20 catches in 1990 to 93 in 1991, leading the league with 1,523 receiving yards to (cowboy) boot. He topped 1,200 yards in each of the next four seasons as well, reaching a career high in 1995 with 1,603, while also setting career highs with 111 catches and 10 TDs. He capped that season off by helping the Cowboys win Super Bowl XXX and complete their remarkable run.

Irvin brought impressive flair and an oversized personality to a Cowboys team still coming out of the long shadow of the more vanilla years of Tom Landry and Roger Staubach. If Aikman was the tough but quiet leader and running back Emmitt Smith the emotional center, Irvin was the party king. When the Cowboys were on top, he made sure everyone knew about it.

A serious back injury slowed his high-speed, high-flying game, and Irvin retired after a four-game stint in 1999.

6 POINTS

- Set University of Miami record for career TD catches with 26
- Set NFL record with eleven 100-yard games in 1995
- Caught two TD passes in a span of 18 seconds in Super Bowl XXVII
- Topped 100 receiving yards in a game 47 times
- Second all-time with 87 postseason receptions
- Appeared in Adam Sandler movie *The Longest Yard*

SAM HUFF No. 93

NEW YORK GIANTS
WASHINGTON REDSKINS

POSITION: LINEBACKER
YEARS: 1956–1967, 1969
HEIGHT: 6-1 WEIGHT: 230
SCHOOL: WEST VIRGINIA
HALL OF FAME: 1982

Was there ever a tougher guy in the NFL than Sam Huff? Well, you sure wouldn't say so to his face. In fact, what he famously said he wanted to hear was "Uuurrff!" That is, the sound at the receiving end of one of his fierce tackles.

Not quite big enough to play on the line, but big enough that coaches at first worried that he'd be too slow at linebacker, Huff actually left the Giants' camp in frustration before the 1956 season. At the airport, assistant coach Vince Lombardi talked the West Virginian out of heading home. In the end, Huff turned out to be the perfect blend of both positions. And thanks to Giants assistant coach Tom Landry's new schemes, Huff helped define the position of middle linebacker.

He also found himself at the media center of the world in a position that was beginning to change the game. Huff ended up on the cover of *Time* and as the subject of a CBS documentary called "The Violent World of Sam Huff."

Huff joined the Giants in 1956 in time to help them win the NFL championship. He was on the losing end of the 1958 title game against the Colts, the famous "Greatest Game Ever Played." That season also marked the first of his five Pro Bowl selections. Huff helped the Giants earn a spot in six NFL Championship Games. In 1964, he moved to the Washington Redskins and played for four more seasons. In 1969, he came out of retirement for the chance to play one season under Vince Lombardi in Washington. As it turned out, two of the toughest guys in recent memory headed into their NFL sunsets together.

6 POINTS

- Real full name is Robert Lee Huff; Sam's a nickname
- Was 1955 All-America while playing offensive guard and defensive tackle
- Returned two fumbles and two interceptions for TDs
- Intercepted 30 passes in his career
- Named NFL's top linebacker in 1959
- Grew up in West Virginia in a row house with no running water

LENNY MOORE
BALTIMORE COLTS

POSITION: RUNNING BACK
YEARS: 1956–1967
HEIGHT: 6-1 WEIGHT: 191
SCHOOL: PENN STATE
HALL OF FAME: 1975

I f you look at some of the numbers, Lenny Moore did not have an impressive career. He never gained 1,000 yards in a season either rushing or receiving. He only had fifty catches in a season once.

But you'd be looking at the wrong numbers.

Moore led the NFL four times in yards-per-carry, topping seven yards three times. He scored 10 or more total touchdowns in five seasons, including an NFL-leading 19 in 1964. He scored a touchdown in an NFL-record 18 straight games in 1964–65. His 113 total touchdowns put him second at the time behind only the great Jim Brown.

Moore for the score: That was a huge part of the Baltimore Colts offense for more than a decade. Fellow Colts star Raymond Berry called Moore "the greatest scoring weapon" he had ever seen.

Moore was a superstar as a running back at Penn State, but upon moving to the NFL, he had to define a new role for himself. He was not quite tall enough to be a full-time flanker, nor heavy enough to take the pounding meted out to running backs by NFL bruisers. Wisely, the Colts recognized in this speedy, elusive runner a special talent. He became a perfect cog in the Johnny Unitas–led offense, most often using his speed for downfield receptions but also mixing in runs as a halfback; he was a sort of early version of all-around backs such as Roger Craig and Marshall Faulk. Moore ended up as the 1956 Rookie of the Year as the Colts made it to the NFL title game.

By 1958, Moore not only led the NFL with a 7.3 rushing yards per attempt, he also averaged nearly 19 yards per catch. That year, he helped the Colts win the first of two straight NFL championships by winning the "Greatest Game Ever Played" over the New York Giants. In that game, Moore caught six passes for 101 yards. What is often over-looked is that it was his amazing 73-yard touchdown run that brought

CAREER STATS				
Yrs.	Att.	Yds.	Yds./Carry	Rush TDs
12	1,069	5,174	4.8	63

the Colts to a comeback victory a few weeks earlier to help the Colts win the Western Conference crown.

Moore was a Pro Bowl–level player every year from 1958 through 1962. Injuries slowed him down, however, and in 1963 he played only seven games. Showing a resolve and toughness that matched his game-breaking speed, he came back to lead the NFL with 16 rushing TDs in 1964 and was named the Comeback Player of the Year. Moore retired after the 1967 season, leaving behind a legacy as one of the best open-field runners of all time, and a player with an almost un-matched nose for the end zone.

- As a defensive back at Penn State, picked off 10 passes
- Led NFL in 1957 with 1,175 yards from scrimmage
- Scored TDs of at least 70 yards in seven different seasons
- Nicknamed "Spats" due to the way he taped his shoes
- Named to five All-NFL first teams
- Only player with at least 45 TD catches and 60 rushing TDs

No. 95 LARRY ALLEN

DALLAS COWBOYS
SAN FRANCISCO 49ERS

POSITION: GUARD/TACKLE
YEARS: 1994–2007
HEIGHT: 6-3 **WEIGHT:** 325
SCHOOL: SONOMA STATE
HALL OF FAME: ELIGIBLE IN 2013

When Emmitt Smith looks up and sees his name atop the NFL's all-time rushing list, he probably has to stand on his tiptoes to see over the man who was in front of him for thousands of those yards. Larry Allen was one of the premier offensive linemen in the NFL for his entire 14-year career, and is considered one of the best-ever guards.

The Cowboys made one of the most prescient picks in NFL history when they snatched Allen from tiny Sonoma State in the second round of the 1994 draft. He quickly earned a place as anchor on a Dallas O-line that helped pave the way to a title in Super Bowl XXX. Four members of that line went to Hawaii for the Pro Bowl. The trip became an almost-annual rite for Allen. With 10 Pro Bowl selections in his dozen years in Dallas, Allen went to more of the postseason all-star games than any offensive player in the Cowboys' long and illustrious history. At the time, Allen, who played both guard and tackle during his career, was only the third player ever to earn Pro Bowl nods at more than one line position. Smith and other Dallas running backs set record after record with Allen blocking, while Troy Aikman might go several games without hitting the turf, thanks to Allen and his linemates.

After 11 seasons in Dallas, he was released in 2006, but signed with San Francisco. There, he helped Frank Gore set a team rushing record. Though he played his last NFL game as a 49er in 2007, he signed a one-day contract with the Cowboys so that he could retire as a member of the team that he had helped for so many years.

6 POINTS

- First Sonoma State player ever chosen by NFL team
- Attended Butte Junior College prior to playing two seasons for Sonoma State
- Selected six times as First-Team All-Pro
- Named to NFL's All-Decade Teams of both 1990s and 2000s
- Reportedly one of NFL's strongest men with a 700-pound bench press
- Played all 16 games in 11 of 14 seasons

MEL HEIN No.

NEW YORK GIANTS

POSITION: CENTER/LINEBACKER
YEARS: 1931–1945
HEIGHT: 6-2 WEIGHT: 225
SCHOOL: WASHINGTON STATE
HALL OF FAME: 1963

Mel Hein brings two legends to his story in the NFL 100. The first is that he had reputedly the biggest hands ever seen, seeming to swallow the bulbous ball used in his era (1931–45). The second is one of those "couldn't happen now" stories that gives the early NFL such a *Wonderful Life* feeling.

Hein was a superstar in college in far-off Washington State. Helped by a Rose Bowl win and a spot on Grantland Rice's All-America team, he had a pretty good reputation. Still, in those days before the NFL Draft, it was more of a crapshoot as to who would end up where. Hein himself actually had to write to three NFL teams asking for a job. The not-long-for-the-NFL Providence Steam Roller answered first, offering $135 a game. Not bad, thought Hein, who dropped off a letter agreeing to roll with Providence. Later the same day, a Giants coach came in person with a better offer: $150. Thanks to a helpful postmaster who held up the letter to Providence, the Giants ended up with Hein's services.

And they were sure glad they did. As a two-way player at center and linebacker, Hein was named All-NFL eight times. In 1938, he became the only center ever named NFL MVP. His best position was on offense, but on defense he was good enough to snag 10 interceptions in his final six seasons, the only ones for which official stats are available.

When the inaugural class of the Pro Football Hall of Fame was named in 1963, there was no doubt who would hold down the center spot: Hein, the 10-year captain and all-time great, with a nod of thanks to the U.S. Postal Service.

6 POINTS

- Also played basketball as a Washington State senior
- 60-minute-per-game player throughout his entire career
- Didn't miss one game due to injury in entire pro career
- Member of inaugural class of Pro Football Hall of Fame
- Coached in pros and college and led AFL officials
- Named to NFL's 75th Anniversary All-Time Team in 1994

97

DERRICK BROOKS

TAMPA BAY BUCCANEERS

POSITION: LINEBACKER
YEARS: 1995–2008
HEIGHT: 6-0 **WEIGHT:** 235
SCHOOL: FLORIDA STATE
HALL OF FAME: ELIGIBLE IN 2014

The first of two back-to-back Bucs in this countdown (the only longtime Tampa Bay representatives), Brooks was one of the NFL's most fierce and dependable defenders throughout his 14-year career. In fact, after starting 13 of 16 games as a rookie in 1995, Brooks didn't miss another start until his retirement after the 2008 season. Thanks to his dominating combination of pass-rushing power and pass-coverage skills, Brooks also was named to 11 Pro Bowls, among the most ever for his position.

Brooks joined the Bucs in 1995 and proved to be the key ingredient in a defense that led the team to its only Super Bowl appearance—and Super Bowl victory—in 2002 in game XXVII. That season, Brooks was at his best, winning the NFL Defensive Player of the Year award. He was an exemplar of the new, post–Lawrence Taylor breed of linebackers, equally skilled at rushing the passer, plugging the run, and covering tight ends and running backs downfield.

But along with his physical skills, Brooks brought an unquestioned air of leadership. When he was on the field, his teammates knew who was in charge. Both by example and emphasis, Brooks helped mold the Bucs into a fierce defensive unit. Off the field, he was perhaps even more respected. Few players of Brooks's era gave as much time and energy to charitable causes. Along with bringing kids to Bucs games as part of the "Brooks Bunch," he took them on field trips to Washington, D.C., and even Africa to show them a wider world.

He'll most likely join fellow Buc Lee Roy Selmon in Canton someday, but the folks at the Hall will have to plan ahead to make sure he has time in what continues to be a busy schedule of helping others.

6 POINTS

- Academic All-America at Florida State
- Won Walter Payton Award in 2000 for community work
- Career-high five interceptions and three TDs in 2002
- Named NFL Defensive Player of the Year in 2002
- Named MVP of Pro Bowl in 2006
- Became fourth player to be selected to 10 consecutive Pro Bowls, win a Super Bowl, and be named NFL Defensive Player of the Year

LEE ROY SELMON No. 98

TAMPA BAY BUCCANEERS

POSITION: DEFENSIVE END
YEARS: 1976–1985
HEIGHT: 6-3 WEIGHT: 256
SCHOOL: OKLAHOMA
HALL OF FAME: 1995

I f there was a silver lining in the Tampa Bay Buccaneers' depressing first season in 1976—when they went 0-14 on their way to a record 26 straight losses—it was that they had made one good move that year: selecting Lee Roy Selmon as the first overall pick in the draft. He arrived from Oklahoma with a stunning pedigree, having won the Lombardi and Outland Trophies in his All-America senior season. A wrecking ball of a pass-rusher, he would give offensive linemen fits throughout his NFL career.

You can't look at his stats to understand his impact; the league didn't even start counting sacks until 1982 (though he did have 78.5 unofficially). The awards, though, speak volumes: six Pro Bowls, four NFC Defensive Lineman of the Year awards, and the 1979 NFL Defensive Player of the Year award.

It was thanks to the Selmon-led defense that the Bucs finally turned their ship around. By his and their fourth season, they made it to the NFC Championship Game. It was a stunning reversal for the expansion franchise, and it helped show off Selmon's skill to the entire league.

Selmon also had the pleasure of playing with his brother Dewey for several seasons on the Bucs. Unfortunately, Lee Roy suffered a back injury that ended his career at the age of 30. The former Academic All-American has been a banker, resturateur, and college athletic director in the years since, but he's still held in esteem as the first Buccaneer in the Hall of Fame.

6 POINTS

- Was one of three All-America Selmon brothers at Oklahoma
- Tampa Bay MVP as a rookie even after missing six games
- Had unofficial career-high 13 sacks in 1977
- Credited with 380 quarterback pressures
- Named co-player of the game of 1982 Pro Bowl
- His restaurants' motto: Play Hard. Eat Well. And Don't Forget to Share.

No. 99 MICHAEL STRAHAN

ny NEW YORK GIANTS

POSITION: DEFENSIVE END
YEARS: 1993–2007
HEIGHT: 6-5 WEIGHT: 275
SCHOOL: TEXAS SOUTHERN
HALL OF FAME ELIGIBLE IN: 2013

Michael Strahan brought an enormous amount of joy to the football field . . . and an enormous problem to opponents. A sack-happy defensive end for the Giants in the 1990s and 2000s, Strahan was a crowd favorite as much for his positive approach and gap-toothed grin as for the ferocity with which he chased opposing quarterbacks.

Though born in Houston, Strahan actually grew up overseas, spending most of his youth in Germany, where his father was stationed in the military. He came back stateside for college and hooked up at small-school Texas Southern. There he earned All-America honors and caught the eye of NFL scouts. The Giants took him in the second round in 1993, and he quickly moved into the starting lineup. From 1994 through 2003, he missed only two games. In 1997, he registered 14 sacks and earned the first of seven Pro Bowl selections. In 2001, he had perhaps his best individual season, leading the NFL with 22.5 sacks. His final sack of Brett Favre gave him the title and also set a single-season record that still stands. He led the NFL again in 2003 with 18.5 sacks. In all, he had six seasons with 11 or more sacks.

Strahan played in two Super Bowls. After the 2000 season, he and the Giants lost to the Baltimore Ravens. After the 2007 season, the Giants faced the New England Patriots in Super Bowl XLII. In a game that remains one of the all-time Super Bowl shockers, the Giants knocked off the undefeated Pats and won 17–14. Strahan had one sack in the game and three tackles.

Not long after that game, he decided to go out on top, retiring with 141.5 sacks, fifth all-time. Bringing his distinctive look and outgoing personality, Strahan has found a home on the small screen. Along with hosting several sports and reality shows, he has become a popular football analyst and has appeared in numerous commercials.

CAREER STATS			
Yrs.	Sacks	Int.	FR
15	141.5	4	15

Taking advantage of his greatest skill, he is seen in one spot "sacking" Donovan McNabb, followed by that big smile that assures viewers he was just having fun. Next up for Strahan might be more national fame: He says he has his eye on Regis Philbin's spot on morning TV.

6 POINTS

- First-team All-Pro four times
- Scored TDs on two interceptions and one fumble return
- Had six seasons with 11 or more sacks
- Named NFL Defensive Player of the Year for 2001
- Played every game from 1996 to 2003
- Has become popular commercial pitchman and TV commentator

JOE NAMATH

NEW YORK JETS
LOS ANGELES RAMS

POSITION: QUARTERBACK
YEARS: 1965–1977
HEIGHT: 6-2 WEIGHT: 200
SCHOOL: ALABAMA
HALL OF FAME: 1985

roadway Joe. Joe Willie. The white shoes. The eye-black. The fur coats, nightclubs, and Fu Manchu mustache.

The Guarantee.

Shorthand versions of Joe Namath such as these defined him to most football fans, from his flashy off-the-field style to his brash personality. Often lost amid the pre-Internet hype that followed him throughout his career were his lightning arm and his almost-scary toughness. On the field, to his teammates, Namath was not the high-paid celebrity QB; he was a fierce leader who earned his fellow Jets' respect with his ability to lead them and to battle through pain to win. Namath went through four knee surgeries in the pre-arthroscopic era, played in pain game after game, hobbled until the end, but never gave up. He was Broadway Joe to the fans. But to the players, he was just Joe.

Being a star was nothing new to Namath. In high school in Beaver Falls in western Pennsylvania (an area famed as a cradle of QBs), he didn't lose a game as a senior. He was also good enough in baseball to field an offer to sign with six different clubs. At Alabama under Bear Bryant, he was outstanding, going 28-3 in three seasons. In his senior year, 1964, the Crimson Tide won the SEC title and the national championship. Next stop: The pros, but with a difference.

Namath came to pro football with the powerful weight of expectations brought about by an interleague rivalry. The AFL Jets were looking for a blockbuster, a star they could ride in their ongoing struggle to overtake the NFL. In the smart-aleck, rocket-armed kid from Alabama, they found their man. Choosing him No. 1 overall in 1965, the Jets won a bidding war with the St. Louis Cardinals for Namath. Along with his salary (of a then-amazing $400,000 contract), they tossed in a Lincoln Continental and scouting jobs for some relatives. It was a simpler time. The Jets' offer, and the chance to play in New York City, lured

CAREER STATS				
Yrs.	W-L	Yds.	TD	Rating
13	62-63-4	27,663	173	65.5

Namath away from the NFL and immediately made him the centerpiece of the league.

He quickly proved to be worth all the hype, leading the AFL in passing yards twice and carrying the Jets to the league title in his fourth season. Though he had already made a big name for himself with his arm and his leadership, in the week before Super Bowl III, he made himself a legend. Early in the week, from the dais at a crowded touchdown-club smoker, Namath broke a cardinal rule of sports: he bragged ahead of time.

"We'll win," he told a surprised audience. "I guarantee it."

As the saying goes, it ain't bragging if you back it up. In what became perhaps the signature moment in the NFL in the past 50 years, Namath's amazingly underdog Jets beat the mighty Baltimore Colts in Super Bowl III, 16–7. Namath did enough in the game to keep the Jets moving, completing 17 of 28 passes for 206 yards. He didn't

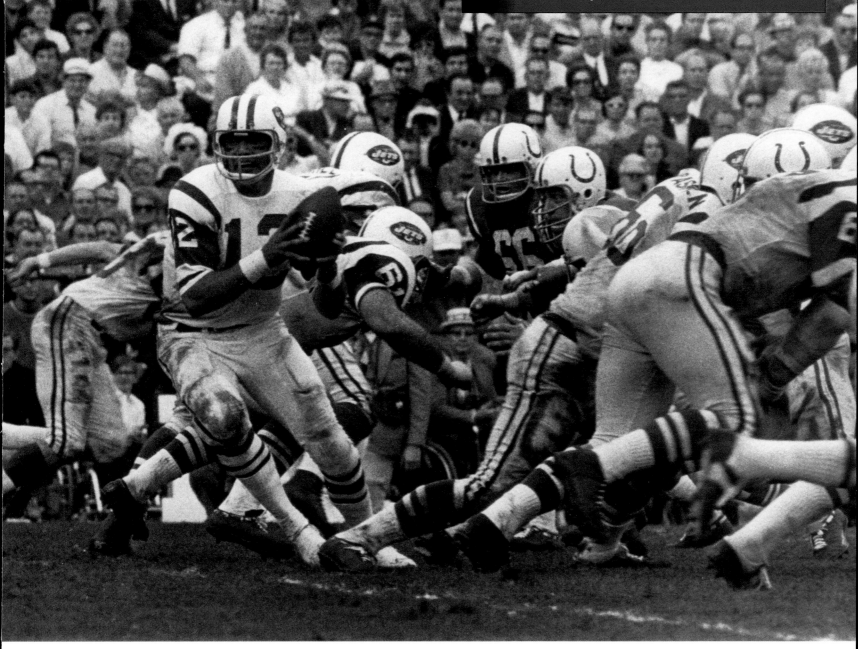

have a TD pass, but he didn't need one. The Jets' D was awesome, while the Colts were uncharacteristically timid and sloppy, throwing four interceptions.

Namath's legend was cemented that day, but his reputation for toughness was one that he ground out game after game.

TOP 100 NFL'S GREATEST PLAYERS BY POSITION

OFFENSE

QUARTERBACK

PLAYER	RANK
Joe Montana	4
Johnny Unitas	6
Peyton Manning	8
Sammy Baugh	14
Otto Graham	16
Brett Favre	20
Tom Brady	21
John Elway	23
Dan Marino	25
Sid Luckman	33
Roger Staubach	46
Bart Starr	51
Terry Bradshaw	50
Troy Aikman	80
Steve Young	81
Norm Van Brocklin	83
Kurt Warner	90
Fran Tarkenton	91
Joe Namath	100

RUNNING BACK/FULLBACK

PLAYER	RANK
Jim Brown	2
Walter Payton	5
Barry Sanders	17
Bronko Nagurski	19
Gale Sayers	22
Emmitt Smith	28
Jim Thorpe	37
O.J. Simpson	40
Red Grange	48
Earl Campbell	55
Eric Dickerson	52
Steve Van Buren	58
LaDainian Tomlinson	61
Marshall Faulk	70
Marion Motley	74
Tony Dorsett	77
Marcus Allen	85
Ernie Nevers	89
Lenny Moore	94

WIDE RECEIVER

PLAYER	RANK
Jerry Rice	1
Don Hutson	9
Raymond Berry	36
Lance Alworth	38
Randy Moss	65
Paul Warfield	71
Elroy "Crazylegs" Hirsch	87
Michael Irvin	92

TIGHT END

PLAYER	RANK
John Mackey	42
Tony Gonzalez	45
Mike Ditka	59
Kellen Winslow	67
Ozzie Newsome	73

TACKLE

PLAYER	RANK
Anthony Muñoz	12
Jim Parker	32
Forrest Gregg	54
Jonathan Ogden	72
Art Shell	76

CENTER

PLAYER	RANK
Jim Otto	63
Mike Webster	68
Mel Hein	96

GUARD

PLAYER	RANK
John Hannah	24
Gene Upshaw	56
Bruce Matthews	78
Larry Allen	95

DEFENSE

MIDDLE LINEBACKER

PLAYER	RANK
Dick Butkus	10
Ray Lewis	18
Jack Lambert	29
Chuck Bednarik	35
Ray Nitschke	47
Willie Lanier	53
Mike Singletary	57
Joe Schmidt	84
Sam Huff	93

END

PLAYER	RANK
Reggie White	7
Deacon Jones	15
Bruce Smith	31
Gino Marchetti	39
Willie Davis	86
Lee Roy Selmon	98
Michael Strahan	99

CORNERBACK

PLAYER	RANK
Night Train Lane	30
Deion Sanders	34
Rod Woodson	41
Mel Blount	44
Mike Haynes	49
Herb Adderley	64
Willie Brown	66
Darrell Green	75

SAFETY

PLAYER	RANK
Ronnie Lott	11
Emlen Tunnell	79
Ed Reed	88

OUTSIDE LINEBACKER

PLAYER	RANK
Lawrence Taylor	3
Jack Ham	60
Bobby Bell	69
Ted Hendricks	82
Derrick Brooks	97

TACKLE

PLAYER	RANK
Joe Greene	13
Bob Lilly	26
Merlin Olsen	27
Alan Page	43
Randy White	62

NOTE: NO PLACEKICKERS OR PUNTERS ARE INCLUDED IN THE NFL'S TOP 100

TOP 100 NFL'S GREATEST PLAYERS BY DECADE

1920s

PLAYER	RANK
Jim Thorpe	37
Red Grange	48
Ernie Nevers	89

1930s

PLAYER	RANK
Don Hutson	9
Sammy Baugh	14
Bronko Nagurski	19
Sid Luckman	33
Mel Hein	96

1940s

PLAYER	RANK
Otto Graham	16
Chuck Bednarik	35
Steve Van Buren	58
Marion Motley	74
Emlen Tunnell	79
Norm Van Brocklin	83
Elroy "Crazylegs" Hirsch	87

1950s

PLAYER	RANK
Jim Brown	2
Johnny Unitas	6
Night Train Lane	30
Jim Parker	32
Raymond Berry	36
Gino Marchetti	39
Ray Nitschke	47
Forrest Gregg	54
Bart Starr	51
Joe Schmidt	84
Willie Davis	86
Sam Huff	93
Lenny Moore	94

1960s

PLAYER	RANK
Dick Butkus	10
Joe Greene	13
Deacon Jones	15
Gale Sayers	22
Bob Lilly	26
Merlin Olsen	27
O.J. Simpson	40
Alan Page	43
John Mackey	42
Lance Alworth	38
Roger Staubach	46
Gene Upshaw	56
Willie Lanier	53
Mike Ditka	59
Jim Otto	63
Herb Adderley	64
Willie Brown	66
Bobby Bell	69
Paul Warfield	71
Art Shell	76
Ted Hendricks	82
Fran Tarkenton	91
Joe Namath	100

1970s

PLAYER	RANK
Joe Montana	4
Walter Payton	5
John Hannah	24
Jack Lambert	29
Mel Blount	44
Mike Haynes	49
Earl Campbell	55
Jack Ham	60
Terry Bradshaw	50
Randy White	62
Kellen Winslow	67
Mike Webster	68
Ozzie Newsome	73
Tony Dorsett	77
Lee Roy Selmon	98

1980s		1990s		2000s	
PLAYER	**RANK**	**PLAYER**	**RANK**	**PLAYER**	**RANK**
Jerry Rice	1	Peyton Manning	8	Tom Brady	21
Lawrence Taylor	3	Ray Lewis	18	LaDainian Tomlinson	61
Reggie White	7	Brett Favre	20	Ed Reed	88
Ronnie Lott	11	Emmitt Smith	28		
Anthony Muñoz	12	Tony Gonzalez	45		
Barry Sanders	17	Randy Moss	65		
John Elway	23	Marshall Faulk	70		
Dan Marino	25	Jonathan Ogden	72		
Bruce Smith	31	Kurt Warner	90		
Deion Sanders	34	Larry Allen	95		
Rod Woodson	41	Derrick Brooks	97		
Mike Singletary	57	Michael Strahan	99		
Eric Dickerson	52				
Darrell Green	75				
Bruce Matthews	78				
Troy Aikman	80				
Steve Young	81				
Marcus Allen	85				
Michael Irvin	92				

NOTE: PLAYERS ARE LISTED DURING THE DECADE THEY DEBUTED

TOP 100 NFL'S GREATEST PLAYERS BY TEAM

CHICAGO BEARS

PLAYER	RANK
Walter Payton	5
Dick Butkus	10
Bronko Nagurski	19
Gale Sayers	22
Sid Luckman	33
Red Grange	48
Mike Singletary	57
Mike Ditka	59

DALLAS COWBOYS

PLAYER	RANK
Bob Lilly	26
Emmitt Smith	28
Roger Staubach	46
Randy White	62
Tony Dorsett	77
Troy Aikman	80
Michael Irvin	92
Larry Allen	95

BALTIMORE/INDIANAPOLIS COLTS

PLAYER	RANK
Johnny Unitas	6
Peyton Manning	8
Jim Parker	32
Raymond Berry	36
Gino Marchetti	39
John Mackey	42
Lenny Moore	94

OAKLAND RAIDERS

PLAYER	RANK
Mike Haynes	49
Gene Upshaw	56
Jim Otto	63
Willie Brown	66
Art Shell	76
Ted Hendricks	82
Marcus Allen	85

PITTSBURGH STEELERS

PLAYER	RANK
Joe Greene	13
Jack Lambert	29
Rod Woodson	41
Mel Blount	44
Jack Ham	60
Terry Bradshaw	50
Mike Webster	68

GREEN BAY PACKERS

PLAYER	RANK
Don Hutson	9
Brett Favre	20
Ray Nitschke	47
Forrest Gregg	54
Bart Starr	51
Herb Adderley	64
Willie Davis	86

LOS ANGELES/ST. LOUIS RAMS

PLAYER	RANK
Deacon Jones	15
Merlin Olsen	27
Eric Dickerson	52
Marshall Faulk	70
Kurt Warner	90
Elroy "Crazylegs" Hirsch	87

CLEVELAND BROWNS

PLAYER	RANK
Jim Brown	2
Otto Graham	16
Paul Warfield	71
Ozzie Newsome	73
Marion Motley	74

NEW YORK GIANTS

PLAYER	RANK
Lawrence Taylor	3
Emlen Tunnell	79
Mel Hein	96
Sam Huff	93
Michael Strahan	99

PHILADELPHIA EAGLES

PLAYER	RANK
Reggie White	7
Chuck Bednarik	35
Steve Van Buren	58
Norm Van Brocklin	83

SAN FRANCISCO 49ERS

PLAYER	RANK
Jerry Rice	1
Joe Montana	4
Ronnie Lott	11
Steve Young	81

CHICAGO CARDINALS

PLAYER	RANK
Night Train Lane	30
Jim Thorpe	37
Ernie Nevers	89

MINNESOTA VIKINGS

PLAYER	RANK
Alan Page	43
Randy Moss	65
Fran Tarkenton	91

BALTIMORE RAVENS

PLAYER	RANK
Ray Lewis	18
Jonathan Ogden	72
Ed Reed	88

KANSAS CITY CHIEFS

PLAYER	RANK
Tony Gonzalez	45
Willie Lanier	53
Bobby Bell	69

SAN DIEGO CHARGERS

PLAYER	RANK
Lance Alworth	38
LaDainian Tomlinson	61
Kellen Winslow	67

TAMPA BAY BUCCANEERS

PLAYER	RANK
Derrick Brooks	97
Lee Roy Selmon	98

DETROIT LIONS

PLAYER	RANK
Barry Sanders	17
Joe Schmidt	84

WASHINGTON REDSKINS

PLAYER	RANK
Sammy Baugh	14
Darrell Green	75

BUFFALO BILLS

PLAYER	RANK
Bruce Smith	31
O.J. Simpson	40

NEW ENGLAND PATRIOTS

PLAYER	RANK
Tom Brady	21
John Hannah	2

HOUSTON OILERS

PLAYER	RANK
Earl Campbell	55

ATLANTA FALCONS

PLAYER	RANK
Deion Sanders	34

CINCINNATI BENGALS

PLAYER	RANK
Anthony Muñoz	12

DENVER BRONCOS

PLAYER	RANK
John Elway	23

MIAMI DOLPHINS

PLAYER	RANK
Dan Marino	25

NEW YORK JETS

PLAYER	RANK
Joe Namath	100

NOTE: PLAYERS ARE LISTED UNDER THE TEAM WITH WHICH THEY HAD THE GREATEST IMPACT

INDEX

IMAGE CREDITS

Front cover: ISP/Veer

Back cover and jacket (left to right):
AP Photo/Paul Spinelli, AP Photo/
John Swart, NFL Photos via AP
Images

Front and back endpapers: Danny E
Hooks/Shutterstock.com

Pages 4–5: Photo by Robert Riger/
Getty Images

Page 6: NFL Photos via AP Images

Page 7: NFL Photos via AP Images

Pages 10–11: AP Photo/Greg Trott

Page 11: AP Photo/Greg Trott

Page 12: Photo by Frank Rippon/Getty
Images

Page 13 (top): Photo by Tony Tomsic/
Getty Images

Page 13 (bottom): Photo by Bob
Gomel/Time & Life Pictures/Getty
Images

Page 14: NFL Photos via AP Images

Page 15: AP Photo/Greg Trott

Pages 16–17: AP Photo/Greg Trott

Page 17 (bottom): AP Photo/Greg
Trott

Page 18: NFL Photos via AP Images

Page 19 (left): AP Photo/John Swart

Page 19 (right): AP Photo/Fred Jewell

Page 20: NFL Photos via AP Images

Page 21: AP Photo/John Rous

Page 22: AP Photo/David Stluka

Page 23: NFL Photos via AP Images

Page 24: AP Photo/Darron Cummings

Page 25 (top): AP Photo/Matt Slocum

Page 25 (bottom): AP Photo/Phil
Coale

Page 26: AP Photo/John Lindsay

Page 27: AP Photo/Carl Linde

Page 28: AP Photo

Page 29: NFL Photos via AP Images

Page 30 (clockwise from top): NFL
Photos via AP Images, NFL
Photos via AP Images, AP Photo/
Greg Trott, AP Photo/Mark
Lennihan

Page 31 (clockwise from top): Photo
by Vic Stein/Getty Images, AP
Photo/Richard Drew, NFL Photos
via AP Images, AP Photo/Paul
Spinelli, AP Photo/Gene Puskar,
AP Photo/Rob Carr

Page 32: NFL Photos via AP Images

Page 33 (top): AP Photo/Bill Beattie

Page 33 (bottom): NFL Photos via AP
Images

Page 34: NFL Photos via AP Images

Page 35 (top): NFL Photos via AP
Images

Page 35 (bottom): NFL Photos via AP
Images

Page 36: AP Photo

Page 37: AP Photo

Page 38: Pro Football Hall of Fame via
AP Images

Page 39: NFL Photos via AP Images

Page 40: NFL Photos via AP Images

Page 41 (top): NFL Photos via AP
Images

Page 41 (bottom): NFL Photos via AP
Images

Page 42: Photo by Frank Hurley/
NY Daily News Archive via Getty
Images

Page 43: Pro Football Hall of Fame via
AP Images

Page 44: NFL Photos via AP Images

Page 45: AP Photo/Greg Trott

Page 46: AP Photo/David Drapkin

Page 47: AP Photo/Nick Wass

Pages 48–49: Photo by Bruce Bennett
Studios/Getty Images

Page 49 (bottom): Photo by New York
Times Co./Getty Images

Pages 50–51: AP Photo/Morry Gash

Page 51 (bottom): AP Photo/David
Stluka

Page 52 (clockwise from top): AP
Photo/Phil Meyers, NFL Photos
via AP Images, Photo by Frank
Rippon/Getty Images, AP Photo/
Tom Gannam

Page 53 (clockwise from top): Pro
Football Hall of Fame via AP
Images, Getty Images, NFL
Photos via AP Images, Photo by
James Drake /Sports Illustrated/
Getty Images, Photo by Charles
Aqua Viva/Getty Images, AP
Photo/Rusty Kennedy

Page 54: AP Photo/Paul Spinelli

Page 55: AP Photo/Eric Gay

Page 56: Pro Football Hall of Fame via
AP Images

Page 57: AP Photo/Eric Gay

Page 58: NFL Photos via AP Images

Page 59: AP Photo/Jane Rudolph

Page 60: AP Photo

Page 61: NFL Photos via AP Images

Page 62: AP Photo/Mike Fiala

Page 63: AP Photo/Greg Trott

Page 64: NFL Photos via AP Images

Page 65: NFL Photos via AP Images

Page 66: AP Photo/Kevin Higley, File

Page 67 (left): AP Photo/Bill Kostroun

Page 67 (right): AP Photo/Kevin Rivoli

Page 68 (clockwise from top): AP
Photo/Paul Sancya, AP Photo/
Lennox McLennon, NFL Photos
via AP Images, AP Photo/Ed
Reinke

Page 69 (clockwise from top): AP
Photo/Hans Deryk, AP Photo/
Bob Galbraith, NFL Photos via
AP Images, AP Photo/Charles
Bennett, File, NFL Photos via AP
Images, AP Photo/Paul Spinelli

Page 70: NFL Photos via AP Images

Page 71: Photo by Vic Stein /Getty
Images

Page 73 (left): AP Photo/Rusty
Kennedy

Page 73 (right): AP Photo/LM Otero

Page 74: NFL Photos via AP Images

Page 75: NFL Photos via AP Images

Page 76: NFL Photos via AP Images

Page 77: NFL Photos via AP Images

Page 78: NFL Photos via AP Images

Page 79: Photo by Frank Rippon/Getty
Images

Page 80 (clockwise from top): AP
Photo, NFL Photos via AP Images,
NFL Photos via AP Images, AP
Photo/Paul Spinelli

Page 81 (clockwise from top): AP
Photo/Evan Pinkus, AP Photo, AP
Photo/David Stluka, AP Photo/
Gail Burton/File, Photo by B
Bennett/Getty Images, AP Photo/
Rusty Kennedy

Page 82: NFL Photos via AP Images

Page 83: AP Photo/Jeff Glidden, File

Page 84: NFL Photos via AP Images

Page 85: NFL Photos via AP Images

Page 86: AP Photo/R.C. Greenawalt

Page 87 (top): NFL Photos via AP
Images

Page 87 (bottom): NFL Photos via AP
Images

Page 88: AP Photo/Lenny Ignelzi

Page 89: NFL Photos via AP Images

Page 90: NFL Photos via AP Images

Page 91: Photo by MLB Photos via
Getty Images

Page 92: NFL Photos via AP Images

Page 93: NFL Photos via AP Images

Page 94 (clockwise from top): Photo
by Nate Fine/Getty Images, Photo
by Nate Fine/Getty Images, AP
Photo/Paul Spinelli, AP Photo

Page 95 (clockwise from top): AP
Photo/Jeff Glidden, Pro Football
Hall of Fame via AP Images, NFL
Photos via AP Images, AP Photo/
Mark Duncan, Photo by Vernon
Biever/Getty Images, NFL Photos
via AP Images

Page 96: NFL Photos via AP Images

Page 97: AP Photo

Page 98: NFL Photos via AP Images

Page 99: AP Photo

Page 100: AP Photo/William Straeter

Page 101: AP Photo

Page 102: AP Photo/Ed Kolenovsky

Page 103: Photo by Lou Witt/Getty
Images

Page 104: NFL Photos via AP Images

Page 105: AP Photo/David Stluka

Page 106: NFL Photos via AP Images

Page 107: NFL Photos via AP Images

Page 108: Photo by George
Gojkovich/Getty Images

Pages 110–111: AP Photo/Paul Spinelli

Page 111 (bottom): AP Photo/Chris
Carlson

Page 112: NFL Photos via AP Images

Page 113: Photo by James Flores/
Getty Images

Page 114: Photo by Walter Iooss Jr. /
Sports Illustrated/Getty Images

Page 115: AP Photo/John Bazemore

Page 116: NFL Photos via AP Images

Page 117: Photo by Al
Messerschmidt/Getty Images

Page 118: NFL Photos via AP Images

Page 119: NFL Photos via AP Images
Page 120: AP Photo/Leon Algee
Page 121: AP Photo/Paul Spinelli
Page 122: NFL Photos via AP Images
Page 123: AP Photo/Chris Gardner
Page 124 (clockwise from top): NFL
    Photos via AP Images, AP Photo/
    David Stluka, AP Photo/Paul
    Spinelli, AP Photo/Paul Spinelli
Page 125 (clockwise from top):
    NFL Photos via AP Images, NFL
    Photos via AP Images, AP Photo/
    Bill Kostroun, NFL Photos via
    AP Images, NFL Photos via AP
    Images, AP Photo/Bill Kostroun
Page 126: AP Photo/Rob Burns
Page 127: AP Photo
Page 128: AP Photo/Doug Mills
Page 129: NFL Photos via AP Images
Page 130: AP Photo/George Widman
Page 131: NFL Photos via AP Images
Page 132: AP Photo/Wade Payne
Page 133: AP Photo
Page 134: NFL Photos via AP Images
Page 135: AP Photo/Susan Ragan
Page 136 (clockwise from top): AP
    Photo/Greg Trott, AP Photo/Amy
    Sancetta, AP Photo, AP Photo/
    Stephan Savoia
Page 137 (clockwise from top):
    NFL Photos via AP Images, NFL
    Photos via AP Images, AP Photo/
    Paul Shane, AP Photo/Tony
    Gutierrez, AP Photo/Greg Trott,
    Photo by Tony Tomsic/Getty
    Images
Page 138: AP Photo/Greg Trott
Page 139: AP Photo/Werner Slocum
Page 140: NFL Photos via AP Images
Page 141: Photo by Marvin E.
    Newman/Sports Illustrated/Getty
    Images
Page 142: Photo by Robert Riger/
    Getty Images
Page 143: AP Photo/Gene Puskar
Page 144: NFL Photos via AP Images
Page 145: NFL Photos via AP Images
Page 146: AP Photo/Keith Srakocic
Page 147: Pro Football Hall of Fame
    via AP Images
Page 148: AP Photo/Tom Gannam

Page 149: AP Photo/Greg Trott
Page 150 (clockwise from top): AP
    Photo/Stephan Savoia, Photo by
    Focus on Sport/Getty Images,
    AP Photo/John Swart, AP Photo/
    Lenny Ignelzi
Page 151 (clockwise from top): AP
    Photo/John Russell, AP Photo/
    Duane Burleson, AP Photo/Paul
    Spinelli, AP Photo/J. Pat Carter,
    NFL Photos via AP Images, AP
    Photo/Paul Spinelli
Page 152: NFL Photos via AP Images
Page 153: NFL Photos via AP Images
Page 154: AP Photo/Chris Gardner
Page 155: NFL Photos via AP Images
Page 156: NFL Photos via AP Images
Page 157: NFL Photos via AP Images
Page 158: AP Photo/Paul Spinelli
Page 159: NFL Photos via AP Images
Page 160: AP Photo/Jack Dempsey
Page 161: AP Photo/Fred Fox
Page 162: AP Photo/Bill Kostroun
Page 163: AP Photo/Steve Nesius
Page 164: AP Photo
Page 165: NFL Photos via AP Images

ACKNOWLEDGMENTS

Thanks to Craig Ellenport of NFL Publishing for shepherding and championing this project. Thanks to Jim Gigliotti for his writing contributions, and to Matt Marini for his eagle-eye fact checking and stats support. The author would also like to thank Rams star Jack Youngblood for being in the author's own top 10 of NFL heroes. And the author would like to dedicate this book to John Wiebusch, the longtime editorial director of NFL Publishing, whose leadership, vision, and support were such a big part of the author's professional life with the league.